Justice
Without
Law?

Justice
Without
Law?

Jerold S. Auerbach

OXFORD UNIVERSITY PRESS
Oxford   New York   Toronto   Melbourne

OXFORD UNIVERSITY PRESS

Oxford   London   Glasgow
New York   Toronto   Melbourne   Auckland
Delhi   Bombay   Calcutta   Madras   Karachi
Kuala Lumpur   Singapore   Hong Kong   Tokyo
Nairobi   Dar es Salaam   Cape Town

and associate companies in
Beirut   Berlin   Ibadan   Mexico City   Nicosia

First published by Oxford University Press, New York, 1983

First issued as an Oxford University Press paperback, 1984

Library of Congress Cataloging in Publication Data

Auerbach, Jerold S.
  Justice without law?

  Bibliography: p.
  Includes index.
  1. Justice, Administration of—United States.
I. Title.
KF384.A94   347.73   82–3499
ISBN 0–19–503175–X   347.307   AACR2
ISBN 0–19–503447–3 (pbk.)

Printing (last digit): 9 8 7 6 5

Printed in the United States of America

For
Susan

Preface

Most Americans seek justice in law. Some find it. The luster of the legal process radiates the promise of justice. People are persuaded that law will protect their rights, preserve their liberty, and secure their property. When disputants cannot be reconciled litigation structures the melodrama of human conflict within a precise set of procedures for its resolution. Legal ritual, especially at its most compulsive levels of due process, can contain explosive emotions. Society benefits from the formal processing of disputes that otherwise might erupt in public violence or private vengeance. State authority is reinforced by the deference afforded to official symbols of law and order. The idea of a society without courts and lawyers inspires trepidation.

But law and litigation have their darker side. The legal process can be threatening, inaccessible, and exorbitant—usually it is all of these for the least powerful people in society. It is more likely to sustain domination than to equalize power. Litigation expresses a chilling, Hobbesian vision of human nature. It accentuates hostility, not trust. Selfishness supplants generosity. Truth is shaded by dissembling. Once an adversarial framework is in place, it supports competitive aggression to the exclusion of reciprocity and empathy. Litigation can be as bizarre as Alice's Wonderland. (Some of Alice's strangest adventures, after all, occurred in a court of justice.) As a litigant tumbles down the slippery slope into dense procedural thickets, familiar landmarks recede. The journey may even resemble a sudden regression to childhood. There is a new language to learn, for even articulate adults stumble over legalese. Although a lawyer can provide reassuring guidance, *in loco parentis,* the price of protection is still dependence. Even as a dangerous adversary is fended off, the judge looms as a menacing authority figure, empowered to divest a litigant of property or liberty. Autonomy vanishes as mysteriously as the smile of the Cheshire cat.

For many years, in a meandering historical and personal inquiry, I have struggled to understand the ambivalent role of lawyers and law in American society. During a decade of research and writing about lawyers, I belonged vicariously to a profession that I had earlier rejected. (Appropriately, the relationship was thoroughly adversarial.) After *Unequal Justice* was published I was invited to speculate about the "plague of lawyers" that now infests American society. I became fascinated with the opportunity to explore, from anthropological and historical perspectives, the folkways of our legal culture. As I pondered the legalization of American society, I discovered startling contrasts across time and space. Curiosity about alternative possibilities for dispute settlement, in other cultures and in American history, provoked the inquiry that culminated in this book.

I began with some confident conclusions about the possibility of justice without law, even in modern American society. But as I probed historical patterns of dispute settlement, I discovered that I had tapped some of the deepest values of Americans as individuals and as community members. I came to understand a persistent pattern of rejection of lawyers and courts; and, correspondingly, why law flourishes at the outer edge of community, where solitary individuals feel the need to protect themselves against each other. The communitarian vision still endures, if in barely discernible form. But litigiousness more appropriately expresses the dominant values of our individualistic culture. In the end, perhaps, a familiar paradox (restated): If we are not individuals, who are we? But if we are only individuals, where is the community that gives meaning to individual lives? The search for justice without law may provide valuable hints. It has, at least, helped me to understand why I am left with the uneasy question that is the title of this book.

Acknowledgments

The solitude of thinking and writing always is a mixed blessing. One of its cherished rewards is the encouragement from others that makes it endurable. Many people helped me and I am deeply grateful to all of them.

Two institutions were indispensable. The National Science Foundation granted generous financial assistance, which provided the necessary period of uninterrupted time to complete my research and to compose the early drafts of the manuscript that became this book.* The Harvard Law School welcomed me as a Visiting Scholar for the duration of this project, a pleasing affiliation that only troubled me lest the length of my visit inadvertently provide a right of adverse possession. In many ways, however, I was assured that our relationship was entirely amicable.

During the long journey into print, I was the beneficiary of various forms of assistance, guidance, and reassurance. At Harvard, David Smith kindly facilitated my prolonged visit; Heda Kovaly always was caring and supportive; Pete Meehan patiently tolerated my incessant requests; Frank Sander and Fred Snyder invited my participation in their dispute-resolution classes; and the entire ILS

* Some of the ideas incorporated in this book were developed with the support of National Science Foundation Grant SOC 79.09330. Any opinions, findings, conclusions, or recommendations expressed herein are, however, mine and do not necessarily reflect those of the Foundation.

library staff made me feel at home away from home. I received valuable research assistance from several Harvard law students with the wisdom to question their commitments before affirming them: Thomas Alpert, Jonathan Chiel, Armond Cohen, and especially Emily Joselson. Faculty and students, not only at Harvard, but at the University of Connecticut Law School, Boston University Law School, and, at a crucial time, Osgoode Hall Law School, responded generously as I struggled to transform random thoughts into coherent ideas. Portions of this book, in earlier incarnations, appeared in *Harper's*, *The Nation*, and *The New Republic*, whose editors granted permission to reprint. Archivists at the Central Archives for the History of the Jewish People and at the Central Zionist Archives (both in Jerusalem), the American Arbitration Association, and the Jewish Conciliation Board were extremely helpful. Israel Goldstein provided access to certain of his personal papers. Arthur Goren directed me to important manuscript collections in Jerusalem and untangled some mysteries once I floundered there. Rick Abel, Harry Arthurs, Marc Galanter, Morton J. Horwitz, Pnina Lahav, and Nathan Szanton offered encouragement along the way. Gene Dahmen instructed me in the intricacies of legal dispute settlement while enduring my resistance to it. Pearl Rodgers graciously and expertly typed more drafts of the manuscript than she or I care to remember. Nancy Donovan skillfully prepared the Index. Stephanie Golden and Susan Rabiner of Oxford University Press were demanding, and therefore superb, editors. Stephanie, especially, prodded me mercilessly and shrewdly to do more, and to do it better, than I thought possible, while her editorial guidance was unerring. Ben Zion Gold tutored me in some meanings of community. Throughout my struggle to understand the issues that are woven into this book Benjamin Shambaugh was my wisest teacher.

A community of trusted friends listened, consoled, and shared, even as they occasionally took my requests for constructive criticism all too seriously. Although I appreciate their valuable suggestions, and strongly wish to implicate them in whatever virtues this book has, I treasure far more my bonds of friendship with Fred

Konefsky, Stanley Fisher, Avi Soifer, and with Haggai Hurvitz and Marc Feldman (both of whom offered varieties of wise counsel at the most difficult moments). Michael and Judy Rosenthal in New York, and Haggai and Adina Hurvitz closer to home, frequently nourished me with the warmth of their love. Since this is the second book that I have completed with Haggai nearby as my colleague, we both know by now how much I have been fulfilled by his steadfast companionship.

Every parent of siblings becomes an experienced veteran in the wily arts of dispute settlement. Otherwise Pammy and Jeffrey, still bemused by the mysterious ways their father spends his time, properly refrained from permitting this book to intrude upon their own energetic and creative lives (although Pammy, with laudable ulterior motives, contributed valiantly as proofreader when I desperately needed help).

More than anyone, Susan Levin showed me how to resolve conflict with love and trust. That is why this book is for her, with my love.

Cambridge, Mass.   J.S.A.
May 1982

Contents

Justice
Without
Law?

Introduction

The notion of justice without law seems preposterous, if not terrifying. A legal void is especially alarming to Americans, who belong to the most legalistic and litigious society in the world. Surely history supports our enduring legal tradition, stretching back beyond our seventeenth-century origins to the murky sources of Anglo-Saxon common law. It does; but if we can remove our contemporary cultural blinders we can also locate, during three and a half centuries of our colonial and national experience, many groups of Americans who persistently searched for justice beyond law, without lawyers or courts. Indeed, they found it there: within their communities of faith, ideology, or even profit. Protected by their own choice from the reach of formal law, they lived by values that legal institutions could not satisfy. The meaning of their quest is the subject of this book.[1]

In every society there is a wide range of alternatives for coping with the conflict stirred by personal disputes. Litigation is only one choice among many possibilities, ranging from avoidance to violence. The varieties of dispute settlement, and the socially sanctioned choices in any culture, communicate the ideals people cherish, their perceptions of themselves, and the quality of their relationships with others. They indicate whether people wish to avoid or encourage conflict, suppress it, or resolve it amicably. Ultimately the most basic values of society are revealed in its dispute-settlement procedures. Although every society provides institutions for dispute settlement, by no means are these necessarily, or exclusively, legal institutions. Conceptions of the role of law change, and assessments of the advantages and disadvantages of submitting disputes to its processes not only shift, but exist in perpetual tension.

The American pattern of dispute settlement is, and always has been, more varied and complex than our currently constricted legal perspective would suggest. Tucked away in corners of our historical experience are intriguing experiments that testify to a persistent counter-tradition to legalism. In many and varied communities, over the entire sweep of American history, the rule of law was explicitly rejected in favor of alternative means for ordering human relations and for resolving the inevitable disputes that arose between individuals. The success of non-legal dispute settlement has always depended upon a coherent community vision. How to resolve conflict, inversely stated, is how (or whether) to preserve community.

Historically, arbitration and mediation were the preferred alternatives. They expressed an ideology of communitarian justice without formal law, an equitable process based on reciprocal access and trust among community members. They flourished as indigenous forms of community self-government. Communities that rejected legalized dispute settlement were variously defined: by geography, ideology, piety, ethnicity, and commercial pursuit. Yet their singleness of vision is remarkable. Despite their diversity they used identical processes because they shared a common commitment to the essence of communal existence: mutual access, responsibility, and trust. The founders of Dedham (a seventeenth-century Christian utopian community in Massachusetts), Quaker elders of Philadelphia, followers of John Humphrey Noyes at Oneida (a nineteenth-century utopian commune), the Chinese in San Francisco and Scandinavians in Minnesota, and even Chamber of Commerce businessmen easily could have collaborated on a common blueprint for dispute settlement. Sharing a suspicion of law and lawyers, they developed patterns of conflict resolution that reflected their common striving for social harmony beyond individual conflict, for justice without law.

Religious piety persistently sustained a coherent community vision. Ideally, law and religion might complement each other. Each calls upon tradition, authority, and ritual to justify its world view. But the mystical core of religion does not easily co-exist with the rationality of law. In New England congregations, among Quakers and Mormons, and in religious utopian communities, Christian doctrine encouraged alternatives to law. Legal institutions languished while religion legitimated the social order. If there was a dominant vision that inspired religious communitarians it was their yearning for a harmonious society, shaped by a Christian moral code, reinforced by a sense of divine purpose. As long as religion remained the source of moral wisdom, lawyers and courts were superfluous. But once religious intensity waned, Christian communities where legal conflict had been sinful became places where conflict was permissibly expressed in litigation.[2]

The communitarian vision has been sufficiently expansive throughout American history to permit even the most secular, competitive, and materialistic merchants and businessmen to design their own protected enclaves beyond the reach of law. Utopian Christians and mercenary merchants shared the understanding that law begins where community ends. So they developed patterns and institutions of dispute settlement that contained conflict within their own community boundaries—with courts and lawyers as remote as possible. For centuries merchants and businessmen have been among the most outspoken proponents of non-legal dispute settlement. At each crucial stage in the development of commercial arbitration, it represented the effort of businessmen to elude lawyers and courts and to retain control over their disagreements. The familiar patterns of commercial custom were (and remain) vastly preferable to the alien procedures, frustrating delays, and high costs of litigation. Even in the modern era, when business interests have used non-legal dispute settlement to escape the strictures of government regulation, they have expressed a tenacious commitment to communitarian values (in their case, a community of profit). Secular and selfish to the core, they nonetheless have emerged among the most persistent American defenders of alternative dispute settlement. Buried in that irony lies a revealing example of the commercialization of the community impulse in modern America.

Among the most committed practitioners of non-legal dispute settlement were immigrant ethnic groups. From the Dutch in New Amsterdam to the Jews of the Lower East Side of Manhattan, in a wide geographical arc that encompassed Scandinavians in the Midwest and Chinese on the West Coast, some newcomers from other cultures and traditions tried to place their disputes as far beyond the reach of American law as possible. Aliens in a hostile land, they encountered a society whose legal institutions often were overtly biased against them or, at best, indifferent to their distinctive values. Their own indigenous forms of dispute settlement, centuries old in some instances, shielded them from outside scrutiny and enabled them to inculcate and preserve their traditional norms. Ethnic-group dispute settlement often demonstrated a strong preference for community justice over legal due process, which was significantly less benevolent for new immigrants than government officials and legal professionals proclaimed.

Yet for immigrants, as for religious utopians and businessmen, there was persistent tension between courts and their alternatives. The legal system, which ultimately was the arm of the state, discouraged autonomous pockets of resistance to its processes. Law was one of the primary instruments of acculturation; its rapid extension to immigrant communities was a national imperative. This made law appealing to some ethnic groups, as a vehicle to hasten their absorption into American society. But it threatened others, who feared loss more than they anticipated gain. If some immigrant groups (the Chinese, for example) retained their own dispute-settlement institutions to preserve cultural distinctiveness, so others (Jews in New York) modified theirs to facilitate acculturation. The pattern was as intricate as the American ethnic mosaic itself.

To approach community by way of dispute settlement may seem idiosyncratic. But it provides access to a complex, recurrent cultural dialogue: between individual and community; between the dream of harmony and the reality of conflict; between formal legal institutions and their alternatives. Every society experiences this tension. It is important to understand that dispute-settlement preferences are not ultimate choices, but shifting commitments. Even in the most thoroughly legalized society there is likely to be a restless movement over time: between the strictures of the formal legal system and the lure of informal alternatives. To be sure, once the older customary order (based on the shared moral vision of a group) deteriorates, the dominant shift is toward explicit legal rules and procedures "to clarify what the disintegration of community has made dark and slippery."[3] But the benefits of legalism are unevenly (though seldom randomly) distributed through society. Because the cherished social values of some groups cannot be expressed in legal norms, the transition to legality is neither tidy nor complete. It is the unstable equilibrium, particular to time and place, that opens cultural and historical vistas. Communitarian efforts, like the American experience itself, are complex and diverse. Yet there are fascinating patterns, and coherent themes, which dispute-settlement processes can illuminate. The enduring Edenic vision of a harmonious community may invariably be undercut—but even in the American experience, where law reigns supreme, the vision is never entirely stifled.

Communal alternatives to litigation invite consideration of disputation as a form of social behavior. The nature of the disputing process emerges, ultimately, from the delicate interaction of personal relationships within a particular social structure. Whether disputants ignore their differences, negotiate, submit to mediation or arbitration, or retain lawyers to litigate is a matter of significant choice. How people dispute is, after all, a function of how (and whether) they relate. In relationships that are intimate, caring, and mutual, disputants will behave quite differently from their counterparts who are strangers or competitors. Selfishness and aggression are not merely functions of individual personality; they are socially sanctioned—or discouraged. So is the decision to define a disputant as an adversary, and to struggle until there is a clear winner and loser; or, alternatively, to resolve conflict in a way that will preserve, rather than destroy, a relationship. In some cultures, the patterns of interaction suggest that those who participate in litigation may be psychologically deviant. Among Scandinavian fishermen and the Zapotec of Mexico, in Bavarian villages and certain African tribes, among the Sinai Bedouin and in Israeli *kibbutzim* (as in the disparate American communities that are the subject of this book), the importance of enduring relations has made peace, harmony, and mediation preferable to conflict, victory, and litigation. But in the United States, a nation of competitive individuals and strangers, litigation is encouraged; here, the burden of psychological deviance falls upon those who find adversary relations to be a destructive form of human behavior.[4]

Considering some of our historical antecedents, it is the legalization of American society, not the persistence of alternatives, that might seem curious. We know that mistrust of law crossed the Atlantic with the earliest settlers, whose Edenic visions of New World possibilities consigned lawyers to a role only slightly above the Biblical serpent. The *Fundamental Constitutions* of Carolina declared it "a base and vile thing" to plead a case for a fee. Massachusetts and Rhode Island, for a time, prohibited lawyers from serving in their colonial assemblies. Benjamin Franklin's Poor Richard echoed the popular complaint: " 'Tis the Fee directs the Sense to make out either side's Pretense." Colonists referred to a lawyer-bird, with its long bill, and lawyer-fish, always slippery. Yet their suspicion was insufficient to deter the development of a flourishing legal culture. Not long after independence, the Frenchman Crèvecoeur offered his dour description of American lawyers as weeds "that will grow in any soil that is cultivated by the hands of others; and when once they have taken root, they will extinguish every other vegetable that grows around them."[5]

Hostility to lawyers is not, of course, an American monopoly.

In early Greece, republican Rome, and dynastic China there were rules against paid legal advice. Shakespeare's rebel Jack Cade asked: "Is not this a lamentable thing, that of the skin of an innocent lamb should be made parchment? That parchment, being scribbled o'er, should undo a man?" Lamentable though it surely was, lawyers continued to fleece innocent lambs. Modern revolutionary movements—often led by lawyers (Robespierre and Lenin, for example) who were familiar with legal conservatism—quickly moved to eradicate the legal profession. As Cade's fellow rebel suggested: "The first thing we do, let's kill all the lawyers." From an aristocratic perspective, Tocqueville, in his classic exploration of American democracy, shrewdly described the ability of lawyers "to neutralize the vices inherent in popular government." A democratic society, he observed, nurtured the political power of lawyers; lacking an aristocracy, nobility, or royalty, it could only restrain popular turbulence with the conservatism of bench and bar.[6]

Yet by now it is a staple of social commentary to cite the myriad of laws and abundance of lawyers in the United States. Both have proliferated so rapidly as to suggest (even to lawyers) that American society is choking from "legal pollution"; that Americans, as a people, are debilitated by the malady of "hyperlexis."[7] Five hundred years from now, when historians sift through twentieth-century artifacts, they doubtless will have as little comprehension of American legal piety as most Americans now display toward medieval religious zeal. The analogy is illuminating: law is our national religion; lawyers constitute our priesthood; the courtroom is our cathedral, where contemporary passion plays are enacted.

In the twentieth century it is justice, the secular equivalent of salvation, that is sold for a fee. So the cartoon attorney reassures his anxious client about the merits of his case, but inquires, "How much justice can you afford?" Similarly, assertions of lay competence (how to avoid probate without retaining a lawyer) elicit cries of outrage from our contemporary salesmen of indulgences. Efforts to simplify procedure and ease recovery of damages (no-fault insurance) rally lawyers to battle for their fees. Imagine the fate of consumers intrepid enough to suggest that the language of a contract (like the language of the Mass) be subjected to the test of lay comprehension. They might risk commitment, although they would probably have a lawyer at their side to protect their rights (if not their souls).

The problem, of course, goes beyond lawyers, who are creatures of American culture, not its creators. It is, ultimately, a question of values, translated into social structure. In traditional societies roles are defined, stable relationships are developed, mutual responsibility is encouraged, and respect for authority is required. Americans prefer to stand apart, separated from their ancestors, contemporaries, and descendents. Individualism means freedom—above all, the freedom to compete, acquire, possess, and bequeath. It is precisely this freedom that our legal system so carefully cultivates and protects. In a society where the dominant ethic is competitive individualism, regulated by the loose ground rules of the Darwinian struggle (with special protection reserved for crippled corporate giants), social cohesion is an enduring problem. Even as litigiousness expresses, and accentuates, the pursuit of individual advantage, the rule of law helps to hold such a fractured society together. At the least (usually it is also the most), people can agree upon how they will disagree. In a restless, mobile society of strangers, the staple scene of Western movies is perpetually reenacted: an American, at the first sign of danger, reaches for his (hired) gun and files a lawsuit. Yet contradictions abound. Our individualistic society encourages the assertion of legal rights as an entitlement of citizenship, but distributes them according to the ability to pay. Conflict is channeled into adversary proceedings with two combatants in every legal ring; but beyond the implicit assumption that every fight and any winner is good for society, the social good is ignored. Litigation is the all-purpose remedy that American society provides to its aggrieved members. But as rights are asserted, combat is encouraged; as the rule of law binds society, legal contentiousness increases social fragmentation.

Solace lies in the comforting assurance that there is no tolerable, or preferable, alternative. Throughout the twentieth century social theorists have insisted that a formal legal system, with a trained professional class of legal experts, is the superior form of civilized social organization. The transition from unchecked theocratic or secular authority to administration by a legal elite is counted as one of the undisputed blessings in the evolution of modern Western civilization. It marked the triumph of formal justice, with its presumed virtues of rationality, consistency, impersonality, and predictability, over arbitrary rule and social instability. As social fluidity, individual interests, and group pluralism exerted their centrifugal force, legal institutions assured social cohesion, individual protection, and (the ultimate good) capitalist development. They also created the legal culture that now is such a widespread source of public dismay.

Whether the rule of law is perceived as a blessing or a curse, as the highest plateau of civilized achievement or as a disturbing symbol of cultural fragmentation, the role of law in American society is endlessly debated. This is not only because lawyers and scholars enjoy endless debate. Legal norms express a particular cluster of cultural values; legal concepts shape our approach to political and moral issues. In the United States, it is now difficult to frame public issues (or, increasingly, private ones) without recourse to the legal vernacular. Indeed, our culture is so thoroughly legalized that it is difficult for Americans to imagine how any society could be otherwise organized and justified.

In a pluralistic society like ours, liberal ideas and political realities combine to require the balance of competing interests, lest some constituent group feel cheated. The concept of justice loses the clarity it possessed in a communal context. Justice becomes a compromise that gives least offense to the most people. In this setting, lawyers and judges usually are satisfied with whatever results bargaining and negotiation produce; the process, not the result, is their primary concern. (As one judge explained, earlier in this century, justice in a commercial age is "merely a problem of correct bookkeeping.")[8] Any judge who rested his decisions upon independent principles of justice would seem arbitrary and capricious. Yet without a shared understanding of justice, especially between the judges and the judged, disputants become observers rather than participants. Silenced by the language of the law, separated from judges who are conspicuously elevated above the proceedings, disputants have no choice but to become litigants.

The contrast with non-legal disputation has been sharply drawn (by a lawyer): "In the social world, where individuals conduct disputes on their own behalf, they are conscious of creating and affecting the dispute through their own choices. . . . Once lawyers move the dispute into the world of judicial procedure, this perspective changes. It seems to the disputants that the dispute has been taken out of their hands. . . . The client . . . sees the lawyer's actions as representing, not the client's own choices, but rather features of an autonomous proceeding."[9] In any process of dispute settlement that isolates disputants, sets them against adversaries, consigns them to professional specialists, and resolves their disputes according to rules and procedures that are remote and inaccessible, dependency and passivity are likely consequences. Yet Americans persist in the belief that legalization is the benevolent sign of civilized progress.

Perhaps judgment could be suspended on the proposition that law represents progress; therefore, the more of it the better. The consuming American reverence for legal symbols and institutions slights the manifold ways in which law not only reinforces, but imposes, an atomistic, combative vision of reality. "Sue Thy Neighbor" is the appropriate modern American inversion of the Biblical admonition. So a newspaper photograph shows an angry woman, her face contorted with rage, who points menacingly at a cowering man, whose hands are raised in retreat and surrender. A judge looks on impassively, an American flag at his side. "If thy neighbor offend thee," the caption reads, "don't turn the other cheek. Slap him with a summons. And take him to Small Claims Court." It is only a blurb for a television special report, but the line between soap opera and reality is hopelessly blurred. Viewers are promised "a free course in self-defense," evidently a requirement for life among neighbors.[10] (With neighbors like these, of course, enemies are superfluous.) Armed with the sword of litigation, Americans can wage ceaseless warfare against each other—and themselves.

As individuals vigorously assert their legal rights in self-protection, they seldom contemplate their contribution to their own precarious isolation. Nor are they warned that as the blanket of legal protection covers individual rights, state control simultaneously intrudes upon realms once reserved to private choice (when, for example, a fetus may live or a terminally ill patient may die). Inevitably, the very meaning of justice changes: without the universalist content it possessed when community members shared a common value system, it fragments into a set of procedures. A new class of legal experts ascends to prominence, aggrandizing power through its monopoly of legal craft and technique.[11] Then a legal culture is securely in place.

Despite the undiluted praise of its adherents, law raises at least as many questions as it resolves about the nature of the good society. It can provide protection from individual aggression or state intrusion, but it also encourages the isolation that makes protection necessary. Even as it furnishes a thin veneer of community where more substantial supports have collapsed, it elevates personal greed above mutual need. In sum, as one legal scholar has conceded: "The better the society, the less law there will be. In Heaven there will be no law. . . . In Hell there will be nothing but law, and due process will be meticulously observed."[12]

In American history, there are no devils or angels; only people. Some built impressive legal bulwarks against their own worst impulses, or to protect their private possessions. Others designed communities beyond law, and tried to live in them. To be sure, they were often frustrated. One chastened utopian community member concluded sadly: "The Old Adam in us, or the beast, inadequately repressed, made a violent appearance."[13] But the delegalization impulse always survives its failures, just as law inevitably is crippled by its successes. Why? The history of non-legal dispute settlement provides important clues.

In recent years some evident deficiencies of American legal institutions have rekindled the search for alternatives. (The advantages of due process and adversary proceedings always are more evident in a law office or courtroom than in a business office or living room.) Social scientists and lawyers have constructed original theories of dispute settlement. There even is attentiveness to the comparative possibilities offered by other societies. But there is little knowledge of the patterns that American history may encourage, or foreclose. Indeed, law so dominates the way we think that there is not even a satisfactory generic name for our own alternatives—in itself an intriguing commentary. To call them "non-legal," as one must, is still to remain enclosed within the dominant legal categories. (It is as if children were described only as non-adults, or play as non-work.) It is suggestive of the current power of legal modes of thought that alternatives lose their distinctive identity. Instead, they are measured in terms of law and defined by what they are not rather than what they are. Yet these alternatives persist; now, once again, they stimulate a flurry of interest that testifies both to the limits of law and to the yearning for other possibilities. As waves of criticism erode complacency with the legal system, the historical artifacts of our own tradition of non-legal dispute settlement are more evident. From these fragments it is possible to construct a historical model of dispute settlement, one that may provide clues to the current, and recurrent, enthusiasm for alternatives—and to their limitations in our litigious society.

The American historical pattern suggests something more complex than the glorious triumph of law over inferior forms of communitarian extra-legal tyranny. A recurrent dialectic, between legality and its alternatives, is one of our cultural constants —necessarily, it accompanies our tenacious allegiance to the rule of law. Even in the United States, in the modern era, the rapid pace of legalization continues to generate persistent efforts to elude its reach. The high cost and slow pace of litigation, combined with an abiding suspicion of lawyers (if only because Americans are so dependent upon them), constantly feed discontent.

As an overburdened legal system struggles to meet its obligations and fulfill its promises, even legal professionals now join in the chorus of delegalization reform. Bar associations develop mediation projects; the Department of Justice sponsors neighborhood justice centers; scrutiny of the theory and practice of nonjudicial alternatives has become a cottage industry within American law schools. Indeed, lawyers seem so likely to dominate the search for alternatives that only their voices will be heard—and, therefore, no alternatives will be discovered or developed. This is, of course, an appropriate modern American twist: dispute-settlement processes that traditionally were non-legal alternatives have now become thoroughly legalized. The sense of liberation that history provides (which prompted my exploration of alternative possibilities) is checked by the sense of limitations that current developments impose. A movement toward substantive justice, outside the procedural norms of the legal system, has quickly evolved into a movement for procedural reform of the judicial system. A professional community of lawyers and judges has wrenched mediation and arbitration from local communities that once resisted law as an alien value system. Consequently, while the forms of alternative dispute settlement still flourish, its substance recedes to the vanishing point. The relentless force of law in modern American society can be measured by its domination, and virtual annihilation, of alternative forms of dispute settlement.

The tenacious indwelling sense of common purpose that turned communities away from litigation to alternatives like mediation and arbitration is likely to fascinate but ultimately distress modern Americans. It is not easy to empathize with our communitarian forebears. They were too involved in each other's lives to satisfy our craving for privacy and solitude. They were mutually supportive, but also intrusive and suspicious; they were cooperative, but also coercive. The strength of a unified community, after all, implies the ability to compel adherence to its norms, at the expense of contrary individual preferences. The choice of non-legal alternatives to adjudication never was a decision to replace power with love, or coercion with cajoling. It was the application of power to serve the common interest at the expense of competing individual claims. It was, therefore, the exercise of power by the community on its own behalf. This was possible because the meaning of justice was clear to its members. Without that clarity a community could not hope to persuade disputants to respect common needs (often, to be sure, it failed to do so). Precisely that clarity rendered courts and lawyers not only superfluous, but even subversive. Only when there is congruence between individuals and their community, with shared commitment to common values, is there a possibility for justice without law.

An exhaustive survey of the historical evidence of non-legal dispute settlement would indeed be exhausting, but it would not have redeeming value for insight or understanding. The examples in this book could easily be multiplied tenfold—without, however, decisively altering the conclusions. As I learned, fortunately before this book become my life's work, the patterns are more important than the particulars; it is the meaning, not the minutiae, that matters. I have tried to present sufficient evidence to sustain an interpretive analysis, but not enough to overwhelm it. Examples are drawn from every century since the seventeenth, to illuminate broad historical patterns that demonstrate how the processes of dispute settlement express personal choices and, most significantly, cultural values. How Americans dispute tells us something important about who Americans are. Many of our predecessors, through three hundred and fifty years of our history, chose to withhold their disputes from lawyers and judges out of the deep conviction that law subverted more important values that they deeply cherished. Almost nothing is known of their efforts, or the reasons for their successes and failures. Yet amid the persistent debate in our litigious society about the role of law and the preponderance of lawyers, they have something to tell us—not only about themselves, but about ourselves.

Chapter 1

"In Brotherly Affection": Colonial Patterns

Every society searches the past for sources of its present identity. Despite the distortions of time, the bonds of continuity are strengthening. So, with much evidence and some hindsight, it is possible to discover familiar artifacts of an American legal culture early in the seventeenth century. An elaborate, sophisticated judicial and legal system has been located in colonial Massachusetts, within just twenty years of the first settlements. Its presence is indisputable. But legal institutions constituted only part, indeed a small part, of an intricate mosaic of dispute-settlement patterns in the colonies. Disputes were channeled into various institutions, many of which were quite remote from courts and inaccessible to lawyers.[1]

In colonial society non-legal dispute settlement expressed a strong communitarian impulse that was vastly different from anything most contemporary Americans would find familiar, or comfortable. The nature of community varied: most often religious, especially in the seventeenth century, it might also be geographical, ethnic, or commercial. The tighter the communal bonds, the less need there was for lawyers or courts. Colonists who rejected law made a self-conscious choice. They were not a primitive people whose stage of social evolution had yet to reach the "higher" levels of legal development. Rather, as Christians, utopians, Dutch settlers in New Amsterdam, or merchants, they preferred to live within a communal framework that rendered formal legal institutions superfluous or even dangerous. For them law was a necessary evil or a last resort, not a preferred choice. If the colonists seem hopelessly remote, with little to offer our technological society in a secular age, it is worth remembering that they confronted problems of social organization and conflict resolution that are still unresolved in American society. Indeed, some of our contemporary "innovations" in community dispute settlement were already securely established within a few years of settlement—more than three centuries ago.

Colonial dispute resolution often reflected cultural priorities that law could not comfortably express. The first colonists in Massachusetts Bay did not comprehend any social advantages to conflict, or to individual assertiveness. Deviance threatened the stability of their enclosed communities, which claimed the total involvement of members in their common enterprise. Conflict could only weaken the fragile foundations of unity and harmony that supported their existence. The new settlements were too precarious physically, and too enclosed ideologically, for open conflict to be easily accepted. Yet it is axiomatic that group closeness heightens the intensity of conflict. Constantly threatened by the disruptions that their communal intimacy assured, the early settlers preferred to suppress conflict if at all possible. Expulsion and criminal prosecution aside, the only alternative consistent with group harmony was mediation, which turned disputants toward each other in reconciliation, not away from each other in acrimonious pursuit of self-interest. The colonists understood that legal disputation, with its adversarial imperatives, was destructive of the group solidarity upon which they depended for the fulfillment of their mission in the New World. Even schism, inevitably followed by the establishment of a new unified community elsewhere, was preferable to incessant contentiousness.[2] Consequently New England towns often vacillated between the extremes of enforced harmony and open schism. Either conflict was stifled or dissidents departed. Sheer survival in the howling wilderness of the New World demanded nothing less. The middle ground of resilience and accommodation was extremely narrow in the seventeenth century. It did not expand significantly until colonial society lost some of its ideological rigidity and religious intensity.

The first generation of New England colonists comprised a religious people whose covenants with God (and with each other) bound them together in congregational communities where Christian precepts of brotherly love were taken seriously. Tolerance was not a virtue in these communities. Puritans were orthodox Christians for whom the word of God was clear, and clearly stated in the Bible. They left England to escape what they perceived as individual greed, social disintegration, and an impure Anglican Church. Their New World "city upon a hill" was designed to serve as a model for others to emulate. It was a communal prescription, not a geographical description. Society was an organism; its members were part of a social unit dedicated to serving God's will on earth, not an aggregation of individuals. As John Winthrop declared in his sermon on board the *Arbella*, before the Puritans landed in Massachusetts Bay, "We must entertain each other in brotherly affection. . . . We must delight in each other, make others' condition our own, rejoice together, mourn together, labor and suffer together." It is not the fine points of the Puritans' theology, but the tenacity of their perfectionist communal vision, that is illuminating. Their fundamental principle of association, expressed in one typical town covenant, was "everlasting love." It required, paradoxically, exclusion of the "contrary minded"; any "differences" must be mediated by members, not consigned to lawyers. For Zion to survive in the wilderness according to Puritan design, the dispute-settlement framework, like the holy experiment itself, must be communal, not individual. Its spirit was religious, not secular; the style was consensual, not adversarial.[3]

Puritan religious values provided the primary framework for non-legal dispute settlement. For the Protestant dissenters who emigrated to America, Christianity shaped their world view, the church was their central institution, and the congregation was their community. Because religion permeated their lives, it shaped their approach to the problem of conflict resolution. To seventeenth-century Americans our self-evident distinctions between church and state would have been incomprehensible. That separation, defined by its ideological defenders as "enlightenment," lay in the future. Puritans inhabited a unified civil and religious community, a Bible commonwealth. Dissent was an unwelcome intrusion, which only encouraged "unhappy Divisions."[4] Communal harmony was the supreme value; disputes between members threatened the very essence of the Puritan mission in the American wilderness.

Despite Winthrop's admonition, however, New England town life hardly was Edenic; the full range of human conflict was experienced there. When it erupted (as it inevitably did) it was often resolved without recourse to the legal process. Litigation was perceived as a form of self-aggrandizement contrary to the best interests of the community. It was also un-Christian: law, in the words of one minister, was "an heart without affection, a mind without passion." In these closed Christian communities law represented an alien value system, antithetical to Christianity itself.[5]

The centrality of the church in the Puritan communities of Massachusetts can hardly be exaggerated. Blurred jurisdictional lines between churches and courts suggest the fusion of civil and religious authority. The Puritans did not establish distinct ecclesiastical courts. Instead, each church functioned as a court for a wide range of disputes. Jurisdictional purists occasionally quibbled: some insisted that even criminal complaints must first be heard by the church; others cited dangerous consequences if they were removed from civil magistrates. Commonly, however, the untidy boundary between civil and ecclesiastical authority encouraged fluidity. So, for example, church absence on the Sabbath was a punishable civil offense. Slander, theft, or sexual immorality might be resolved by church or court, or both. (Anne Hutchinson was tried by civil authorities for sedition and by the church for heresy.) Offenses that for later generations were thoroughly secular—drunkenness and adultery—were heard by churches as well as courts. A standard array of religious offenses provided the staple of church jurisdiction: defilement of the Sabbath (by work or play), criticism of ministers, and heresy. But churches also resolved a variety of commercial and property disputes. These included questions of business ethics (allegations of cheating and excess profits); land title disagreements; and, as late as the beginning of the nineteenth century, allegations of breach of contract and fraud.

Legal dispute settlement was explicitly discouraged. To sue a fellow church member, according to the Reverend John Cotton, was "a defect of brotherly love." (By order of a Boston town meeting in 1635, no congregation members could litigate unless there had been a prior effort at arbitration.) Puritans worked laboriously to resolve conflict, and restore communal harmony, without the assistance of lawyers. One protracted dispute illuminates the Puritan alternative. In 1640 Mrs. Hibbens, wife of a prominent Boston resident, quarreled with Mr. Crabtree about his fee for carpentry work in her house. Mr. Hibbens proposed arbitration: he chose one carpenter and Crabtree selected another. The arbitrators set a revised fee, but Mrs. Hibbens remained obdurate. Indeed, she complained bitterly and publicly about "brother Davis," one of the arbitrators. (Even Governor Winthrop, at her insistence, came to inspect the work.) The carpenters became incensed at Mrs. Hibbens' aspersions on their skills, which diminished their reputation in the community. Church elders approached Mrs. Hibbens, but she remained unmollified. After another arbitration attempt failed, the dispute moved into the First Church of Boston, where Reverend Cotton presided.

Once in church, however, the essence of the dispute shifted—from a disagreement over wages to the stubborn recalcitrance of a church member who did not respect communal fellowship. In the bitter words of brother Davis, the carpenter: ". . . she did not deal with me according to the rule of the Word . . . in the name of Christ. . . . She never dealt with me." Face-to-face engagement between disputants was a religious and communal obligation, which Mrs. Hibbens had recklessly disregarded by complaining behind the carpenters' backs. In a proceeding that required two meetings, a week apart, and elicited the participation of brethren, sisters, and elders of the congregation, Mrs. Hibbens' conduct was relentlessly scrutinized and criticized. Reverend Cotton reminded her of proper procedure for dispute settlement: it was "a breach of rule that you should entertain such jealousies and speak so hardly of brethren, to their defamation, and yet would not deal with them in a church way, nor labor to bring them to a sight of their sin. And if you could not do it yourself, then to take two or three brethren to convince them of their unconscionable dealing, and if they could not to bring it to the church." The "church way" required a collective congregational effort, not individual self-assertion.[6]

Nothing resembling legal due process existed in church proceedings, which varied among congregations. The accused might bear the burden of proof; a minister might combine the functions of judge and prosecutor; lawyers did not participate; there was no provision for appeal. Instead, the entire congregation participated in a process designed to reassert harmony and consensus. (In Boston strangers might occasionally be granted access.) Congregants were free to offer information, opinion, and admonition, but the purpose of individual participation was to encourage a collective congregational judgment, which would isolate offenders, restore them to congregational fellowship, and thereby strengthen communal values. The sanctions of admonition and excommunication were sufficient for this purpose. The church could neither arrest a wrongdoer nor seize his property, but the danger of expulsion, where church and community were virtually co-extensive, loomed ominously. That was Mrs. Hibbens' ultimate fate. When a collective expression of congregational disapproval was unmistakable, the pastor called for a vote on excommunication. Its power can be inferred from his stern words thereafter: "I do here, in the name of the whole church and in the name of the Lord Jesus Christ . . . pronounce you to be a leprous and unclean person; and I do cast you out and cut you off from the enjoyment of all those blessed privileges and ordinances which God hath entrusted his Church withal, which you have so long abused."[7] Later generations might honor seventeenth-century outcasts for their assertiveness against an oppressive community will. But this is an inversion of Puritan priorities. Expulsion, a dire last resort, reasserted consensual authority and thereby preserved the community against those whose self-assertiveness would subvert it.

Beyond the congregation, New England towns imposed their own dispute-settlement procedures, which provide intriguing examples of the relationship of ideology, theology, land ownership, and commercial development to legality and its alternatives. In Dedham, a community established southwest of Boston in 1636, utopian values reinforced Puritan theology with a perfectionist zeal that virtually eliminated legal adjudication for a half a century. The Puritan founders of Dedham built their venture on the principle of Christian love and harmony, tolerating within their midst only those who were "of one heart with us." As one sympathetic historian has concluded: "The founders saw no contradiction in the idea that the ideal society was to be built upon a policy of rigid exclusiveness." Yet they anticipated internal disagreements and provided in their covenant for an informal mediation system to resolve them. Disputes were mediated by "three understanding men," or by "two judicious men," selected by the townsmen or by the disputants themselves. Mediators urged disputants to "live together in a way of neighborly love and do each other as they would have the other do themselves." Their decisions, rooted in community consensus, were rarely challenged. Not only did Dedhamites resolve their internal disputes without lawyers or courts; they also settled their disagreements with neighboring villages by arbitration, mediation, "or any other peaceable way." For nearly fifty years Dedham villagers lived within a social structure that combined a fierce passion for order with the rigorous Christian theology of English Puritanism. In their utopian experiment legal contentiousness was an intolerable affront, indeed a serious menace, to the unity and harmony which their community relentlessly pursued.[8]

Even where the fervor of Christian utopianism was lacking, other sources of cohesion deterred litigiousness. In Sudbury, a nearby village founded two years after Dedham, patterns of land distribution shaped a community that renounced legal adjudication for nearly two decades. Communal land ownership, rather than Christian utopian ideology, provided the framework for unity. Although Sudbury settlers had experienced a wide range of contacts with English justices of the peace and church courts, they jettisoned familiar legal institutions in their new village. Harmony and order in Sudbury came from communal imperatives, not legal obligation. Land allocation expressed this urge. The power to distribute land was the power to determine the communal, no less than the physical, contours of the town. Villagers came from scattered English towns and parishes, but there was a sufficient commitment to the cooperative principles of English open-field farming for it to be implemented in Sudbury.

Peter Noyes, an open-field yeoman farmer from Weyhill, in Hampshire, was one of three joint recipients of a grant from the Massachusetts General Court to distribute land in the Musketaquid Valley west of Watertown. Under Noyes's guidance, Sudbury townsmen replicated an English open-field village. Once individual plots were allocated to the original settlers the remainder—approximately nine-tenths of the whole—was held in common for the benefit of the entire community. Open-field farming required that the special attributes of a land tract—its meadows, woods, and water—be reserved for common use. Decisions regarding pasturage, fencing, planting, and animal management were common decisions of the townsmen, who met frequently in open town meetings. The allocation of Sudbury land—for people, animals, and crops, indeed for the life of the community—reflected traditional patterns of communal relations whose roots stretched back to feudal England. In Sudbury, as in Weyhill, selfish interests would be sacrificed for the common weal.[9]

For almost twenty years the experiment succeeded and Sudbury was distinguished by its social harmony. Compared to neighboring Watertown, or to contemporary English towns, there is a striking absence of evidence of litigated disputes, either among Sudbury residents or between them and neighboring town-dwellers. If possible, agreement was secured through dis-cussion; otherwise it was achieved by arbitration. During the first eighteen years, only three disputes from Sudbury reached the Middlesex County Court. The record of the sole surviving case to have come before Sudbury judges indicates that even that dispute was sent to arbitration. The virtual absence of judicial activity suggests that disputes were resolved through non-legal channels—or that disagreements were not permitted to surface at all.[10]

The Dedham-Sudbury pattern was not unique in the early years of settlement. The necessity for harmony in the precarious new towns of Massachusetts Bay was widely understood and the achievement of it deeply cherished by their inhabitants. Whether or not these were the "peaceable kingdoms" that some historians have discovered, there is abundant evidence that non-legal dispute settlement flourished—at least in some towns, and occasionally for a substantial period of time. Even in Boston, disputes were at first settled "amicably by arbitration . . . without recourse to law and courts." In 1635 the town meeting ordered that no inhabitants "shall sue one another at lawe" until an arbitration panel had heard the dispute. Lay and church leaders in Boston shared a strong bias against lawyers, whom John Cotton denounced as "unconscionable Advocates [who] use their tongues as weapons of unrighteousness . . . to plead in corrupt Causes."[11] Wherever the distribution of land and authority or religious piety rein-forced communal ideology, lawyers and courts were unnecessary.

Non-legal dispute settlement was not an idiosyncracy confined to the Massachusetts Bay Colony. Several colonies—including Connecticut, Pennsylvania, and South Carolina—experimented with arbitration of disputes (especially debt and trespass) that required quick, inexpensive resolution. The Connecticut General Court advised towns to consider arbitration as an alternative to "unnecessary tryalls by jury." In the independent colony of New

Haven, litigants were urged to settle their disputes, especially "darke" (complex) cases, "in a private way" with friends as mediators. New Jersey also provided for arbitration by "indifferent persons of the neighborhood," to prevent "needless and frivolous" litigation. Virginia disbarred paid attorneys; then it fined lawyers who appeared in court. Its legislature expressed dismay with "excessive charges and greate delaies and hinderances of justice between the subjects of this colony." The same complaints recurred: the common law was too technical; litigation was too costly; lawyers were not trustworthy.[12] The result was a patchwork pattern of non-legal dispute resolution systems, some religious and others secular, scattered throughout the colonies.

Doubtless the best-known example outside New England is the Quakers, another "holy community" whose aversion to litigation expressed their commitment to the "love, order, and unity of the brethren." George Fox, founder of the Society of Friends in England, recalled Paul's admonition: "Dare any of you who have a matter against another go to law before the unjust, and not before the saints?" Friends were urged to avoid lawsuits; their cause might be just, but "the Truth seldom gains ground thereby." They learned "that suits of law never furthered our journey, but rather set us backward." Litigation produced only "baneful results" and "feelings subversive of the very purpose for which religious society was instituted."[13]

For Quakers, as for Puritans, the New World offered a magnificent opportunity for orthodox Christians to design a new society according to religious specifications. As in the city upon the hill in Massachusetts Bay, in the holy community that William Penn and the Society of Friends began to build in 1682 between the Delaware and Schuykill rivers, individuals belonged to a social organism that was designed to do the service of God's will on earth. (Their common purposes did nothing, however, to encourage amity: Quakers proselytized among Puritans, who persecuted Friends who were so foolhardy as to venture into Massachusetts Bay.) For Quakers, divine illumination was personal (whereas for Puritans the ultimate source of religious authority was the revealed Scriptural word). But spiritual wisdom was "a *corporate* affair . . . From first to last *the group was the unit*." Inner truth and corporate worship were not incompatible. In silent Quaker assemblies God was revealed to the group no less than to its individual members. The sense of the meeting was crucial; its importance transcended the potentially atomistic individualism of Quaker Inner Light doctrine. Quakers were not only pious; they were pacifists who were obligated "to seek peace with all men, and to avoid giving provocation or just offense to any." Disagreements should not be resolved by "hot contests," but with "love, coolness, gentleness and dear unity." For Quakers, as for Puritans, contentiousness threatened the very existence of their Christian community. Despite theological differences, Quakers and Puritans shared a keen antipathy to the open expression of conflict. Consequently they shaped remarkably similar patterns of dispute settlement in the interest of group harmony.[14]

Quakers resolved their disputes according to an explicitly defined procedure, known as the "gospel order," based upon Matthew's New Testament prescription. First, the complainant, "calmly and friendly," spoke to the other party, trying "by gentle means, in a brotherly and loving manner to obtain his rights." If he was unsuccessful, he reasserted his claim in the company of one or two other "discreet, judicious Friends," who were expected to act "justly and expeditiously" to resolve all differences. That failing, they were to "admonish and persuade" the parties to accept arbitration by disinterested Quakers. Refusal to arbitrate diverted the dispute to the monthly meeting, which enforced the norms of the holy community. It was determined to avoid "Contention and indecent noise." The meeting appointed arbitrators; refusal to abide by their judgment was an intolerable affront to the entire community. "Such Person must be dealt with as one disorderly, and that regards not peace either in himself or in the church and that slights the love, order, and unity of the Brethren." The penalty was disownment by the society. Only after disownment could an ex-Friend pursue a remedy at law.[15]

The process of dispute settlement, whether invoked by the parties, guided by arbitrators, or imposed by the meeting, was designed at every stage to suppress conflict. As gently as the Friends pursued peace and harmony, however, they did not always succeed. As they moved from their meetinghouses to their countinghouses, combining religious piety with commercial acumen and the pursuit of profit, they were drawn into the legal system. Religious communal doctrine found expression in the meeting, but the contentiousness of the marketplace brought Quakers to court.[16]

Although Quakers did not often litigate against each other, they did appear in court, as both plaintiffs and defendants, in disputes with non-Friends. Quakers comprised the government in Pennsylvania until the mid-eighteenth century. Their judicial system, there as in the Quaker settlement of West New Jersey, was "open, easy, and cheap." No attorneys' fees were required; anyone could plead his own cause. If conflict could not always be suppressed prior to litigation, the pressure for harmonious resolution was evident even after litigation began. At various stages the parties might request arbitration; at times the court ordered it. Arbitrators constantly struggled to reassert the principle of harmony. (One award instructed the disputants that "all quarrels, etc. between the said parties to this day cease." Another set of arbitrators pleaded "for the ending of all differences from the beginning of the world to the date hereof.")[17]

By the early eighteenth century, however, the Quakers found it increasingly difficult to divert their disputes from the judicial system. The pursuit of wealth and power in a more secular age, in communities where newcomers and Quakers intermingled, jarred the balance between piety and acquisitiveness, harmony and conflict, suppression and assertion, individual and community. The rhetoric of love and harmony endured, but even as the holy community remembered its "duty to seek peace with all men,"

Quakers found themselves ever more deeply enmeshed in the formal legal system.[18]

The Puritan and Quaker rejection of legal disputation was nurtured by religious piety and ideological zeal. But beyond Congregational churches and Quaker meetings other colonists, who gathered for common purposes of settlement and work, also resisted the incursions of formal legal institutions. Arbitration flourished in New Netherland, where the Dutch, who recruited immigrants throughout northern and western Europe, built their distinctive ethnic enclave within the most heterogeneous population in the colonies.

For two decades after the earliest settlements in New Netherland the colony (at least to one Dutch minister) resembled a "Babel of Confusion." But during Peter Stuyvesant's long tenure as governor, from 1647 until the English conquest in 1664, the fractious pluralism of the colony was tamed by the power of the Dutch ruling elite. The Dutch legal system, rooted in Roman law, was more tolerant of arbitration than the English common law. So the Dutch leaders, concerned with the spread of litigation "to the prejudice and injury of this place and the good people thereof," established an arbitration Board of Nine Men. Rotating panels of "good men," drawn from the upper stratum of Dutch society, exerted strong pressure for conciliation. As "friendly mediators," they shaped a dispute-resolution system that complemented the Dutch courts. Selected by the court, by disputants, or by the constable, they resolved a wide array of disputes involving debts, wage claims, contractual disagreements, the quality of tobacco, and the disputed disposition of a "sow with shotes." When disputants "set up great claims against each other," arbitrators were appointed by the court "to examine . . . who is in fault," and "to reconcile parties if possible." Recalcitrant disputants who preferred adjudication were persistently returned by the Dutch court to the arbitrators, who were urged to "settle differences to the best of their ability."[19]

During its heyday in New Netherland, arbitration strengthened the cohesion of the Dutch community (beset by internal divisions and threatened by the proximity of Puritan settlements on Long Island). It helped to consolidate Dutch rule during the Stuyvesant administration by concentrating dispute-settlement power in the hands of the Dutch elite, who could control conflict before it erupted in acrimonious litigation. As long as the Dutch retained control of arbitration they preserved a valuable ingredient of cultural autonomy and self-government. Arbitration survived the English conquest of New Netherland, and was even institutionalized by law as a small-claims procedure. By the end of the seventeenth century, however, its frequency diminished as the Anglicization of New York eroded many of the remnants of Dutch culture. The introduction of English common law encouraged the development of a flourishing colonial bench and bar.[20]

Community in colonial America was also defined by trade and commerce. Colonial merchants, like their predecessors in medieval guilds, preferred to resolve their disagreements according to familiar business custom rather than to enter the labyrinth of common-law technicalities and uncertainties. The common law was "too cruel in her frowns," but mercantile practice could be relied upon to expedite dispute settlement without "interruption of the traffick." As early as the seventeenth century, commercial arbitration developed along the New York–Philadelphia axis. Not only were these the major colonial commercial centers; both the Dutch in New York and the Quakers in Philadelphia had their own independent commitment to arbitration. The strong Quaker presence in western New Jersey strengthened the impetus provided by the advantageous location of that colony between the commercial cities.[21]

By the mid-eighteenth century, commercial arbitration was favored by merchants for its speed and low cost. Not only did courts, according to one New York merchant, dispense "Expensive endless Law"; they were slow to develop legal doctrine that facilitated commercial development. Throughout the eighteenth century they were most protective of landed property.

Judges were inclined to monitor the fairness of commercial contracts, often declining to defer to an agreement based only on the
relative bargaining strength of the parties. Not until the end of
the century did they begin to satisfy merchants that they could
comprehend the intricacies of marine insurance, disentangle disputed mercantile accounts, authenticate foreign commercial
transactions, or accept an agreement that rested upon the convergence of private interests rather than an imposed conception
of fairness. Until then, merchants preferred to rely upon their
own dispute-settlement institutions. The quality of a shipment of
flour or herring, like the appropriate compensation for salvaging
a wrecked ship, was best determined by partners in trade and
commerce.[22]

In 1768, the New York Chamber of Commerce established the
first private tribunal in America for the extra-judicial settlement
of commercial disputes. "All controversies," the Chamber insisted,
"are antagonistic to commerce." Merchants preferred informed
business experts, sympathetic to commercial imperatives, to inscrutable judges or ignorant juries. Disputes not only disrupted
business but, when litigated in public, invited the intrusion of
outsiders into private business practices (including trade secrets,
preferential terms for favored customers, or price-fixing). Merchants often valued their commercial relationships (and their
profits) over the assertion of legal rights.[23]

The mercantile critique of lawyers was forcefully summarized
by Massachusetts merchant Benjamin Austin, in a series of newspaper articles published in 1786. Most disputes, Austin asserted,
could be better handled by "impartial *referees*" than by "a long
tedious Court process" in which lawyers injected "false glosses
and subterfuges." If decisions by referees were binding, disputing
parties would have a greater incentive to submit their disagreements to "judicious men" who "can have no sinister views, and
who meet solely for an amicable settlement of the contest." Merchants were "the most eligible" persons to settle their own disputes. Austin worried that lawyers, protecting their own interests

(and fees), stood apart from community interests; therefore, it was "the duty of the community to view their conduct with jealousy."[24]

Neither the rhetoric of harmony, nor even the reality of community, however, could suppress conflict—or litigation—in colonial society. The colonists were a contentious people whose aspirations and struggles encouraged the rapid development of an American legal culture. By the end of the seventeenth century, various intersecting loyalties could surface without destroying the community—because the unitary community no longer existed. As these loyalties—to family, church, work, town—multiplied and crossed, the threat of total disaster from every disagreement receded; for pluralistic societies, which value flexibility and change, can easily accept conflict as healthy. Its open expression is assessed as a measure of vigor, not an index of maladjustment. Basic assumptions are seldom threatened by disagreements where pluralism is the basic assumption (unless, of course, pluralism itself is challenged). It may even be difficult to distinguish tolerance from indifference; all points of view are possible because none really matters.

Once the original bonds of unity unraveled, a cluster of values associated with individualism found ready expression: opportunity, mobility, acquisitiveness. With this transformation came the necessary social context for litigation. If mediation and arbitration tended to express the needs of those who were mutually bound in continuing cooperative relationships, the legal process encouraged the clash of individual differences amid constant jostling for private advantage. The shifting balance between non-legal and legal forms of dispute settlement reflected a growing tolerance for conflict. Legalized disputation served those who asserted claims and rights in a competitive struggle with their adversaries.

Law also provided a new framework for order and authority, inviting colonists to pursue their advantage within its rules and procedures (in this sense, law was an alternative forum, serving a different set of interests than arbitration could protect). Disputing individuals wanted to resolve private claims, not restore communal cohesion. So courts replaced churches and town meetings as dispute-settlement institutions; disputants turned to lawyers, not ministers or mediators. Once easy access to land was restricted by its diminished availability, property disputes could be decisively settled in court. Similarly, judicial decisions could provide a framework for the resolution of economic disputes among merchants, tradesmen, and their customers—who, increasingly, were unknown to each other. As strangers and outsiders became town residents, courts were the only institutions whose rules and decisions could gain common acceptance. As neighborly supervision of private conduct became less tolerable, courts eased the friction between neighbors who were no longer bound by a common moral code. Secular legal institutions had to do what the church no longer had the strength to do. Paradoxically, law encouraged contentiousness while channeling it. The mixed benefits provided by litigation made colonists uneasy even as they went to court more frequently. As one historian has suggested, litigation was to the colonial era what the automobile is now: "Everybody denounces its costs, both financial and social, and nearly everybody resorts to it anyway."[25] The analogy is especially appropriate because law was the vehicle that transported a restless, mobile, competitive people into modernity. In a divided, fragmented society only litigation could assure a measure of stability amid conflict.

The pattern was foreshadowed as early as the first decade of settlement. In Boston, where "a people grasping for the rich opportunities of the New World unavoidably trespassed upon each other," adjudication quickly superseded arbitration. Abundant economic opportunity in that expanding commercial and maritime center encouraged rampant acquisitiveness among people who pulled away from Winthrop's community of brotherly affection. So, too, in the smaller outlying villages. As agrarian communities were transformed into bustling commercial towns, as distinct secular and religious spheres emerged, as sons contested with their fathers (and each other) for land, the communal framework was shattered. Even in Sudbury, where common land was the source of communal power, "joint consent" deteriorated into "joint discontent" over the issue of land distribution. The fathers remained committed to open-field farming, but the sons wanted their own land. Title disputes erupted as the sons were caught between population growth and restricted grants of town land. Sudbury literally split apart under competing land claims: dissidents left in 1656 to establish their own new town of Marlborough. With the old constraints receding (the church, too, was in disarray), traditional legal sanctions, abandoned during the first two decades of settlement, reappeared. Sudbury residents returned to the English common law to resolve the frequent and angry disputes that erupted among them; even the town brought suit (against a recalcitrant widow) to secure title to its land claims.[26]

The same process of legalization occurred in Dedham toward the end of the seventeenth century. There had been earlier harbingers of change: a measure of economic and social stratification, declining church membership, the exclusion of newcomers (in one instance, a group of Scotsmen) from the covenant, the termination of open-field farming. As the generation of founders expired, their vision of perfection receded. Once the corporate unity of Dedham disintegrated, arbitration and mediation yielded to adjudication. In Dedham, as in Sudbury, even the town initiated litigation: in 1687 the town treasurer was authorized to "sue . . . according to law." Lawsuits multiplied as aggressive individualism submerged the communal responsibility of the early years, when mediation had expressed deeply shared group norms. Litigation was more appropriate for the emerging town of diverse and assertive individuals.[27]

Two litigious Massachusetts towns, Plymouth and Salem, provide suggestive comparisons with Dedham and Sudbury, where litigation was explicitly rejected or strenuously resisted during the early years of settlement. Plymouth and Salem were towns divided against themselves. With a high level of commercial activity, religious diversity, and private land ownership, they lacked the cohesiveness of agrarian stability and religious unity that Dedham and Sudbury possessed. They were impelled toward law, at the risk of an intolerable level of unresolved conflict. Legal norms offered the only available framework within which disputants could at least agree to disagree. In Plymouth and Salem law not only measured the extent of community fragmentation; it provided the strongest possibility of social cohesion.

For reasons that still are not entirely clear, the balance between harmony and conflict among Plymouth inhabitants seemed precariously tilted toward discord. There is a curious irony here: the Mayflower Compact, after all, occupies a central place in the American mythology of unity and consent. Yet as Governor Bradford sadly noted in his famous history of the Plymouth Plantation, the compact itself was prompted, in part, by "the discontented and mutinous speeches" of "strangers" on the *Mayflower* who did not share the Pilgrims' mission. (Perhaps Winthrop's *Arbella* sermon was similarly motivated.) Despite the shipboard promise to "covenant and combine ourselves together into a Civil Body Politic," the new settlement was plagued by "discontents and murmurings" while it struggled to survive. So, too, an experiment with cooperative crop cultivation, described by Bradford as an attempt to bring "community into a commonwealth," generated "confusion and discontent." With "every man for his own particular," it was soon abandoned for private farming. Unity of purpose in Plymouth was further undercut by the rapid dispersion of its inhabitants. Barren land made farming difficult and drove people away. But, as Bradford complained, "it was not for want or necessity so much that they removed as for the enriching of themselves." Once again, private pursuits seem to have subverted public purpose. As the unity and strength of the town waned, the bonds of religious unity also slackened. Bradford's poignant metaphor captured the loss: "And thus was this poor church left, like an ancient mother grown old and forsaken of her children."[28]

Plymouth was more tolerant of religious diversity (especially the presence of Quakers) than the towns of Massachusetts Bay.

But religious dissent encouraged litigation. Churches could only resolve the disputes of members; dissenters had an obvious interest in seeking the judgment of an independent secular tribunal. By the early eighteenth century in Plymouth County, interdenominational disputes and schism within the Congregational church were contributing to an increase in litigation. Not only were Congregationalists and Quakers going to court against each other, but the monthly meeting had eased constraints against lawsuits between Quakers. Ironically, the Quakers accounted for a disproportionately large share of litigation; an indication, perhaps, of their marginal status in Plymouth.[29]

The conspicuous role of Plymouth as the commercial center of the county may have encouraged the tendency of inhabitants to litigate. By glorifying individual gain, commercial values contributed additional centrifugal force to a community already fragmented by individualism and sectarianism. As commercial activity multiplied relationships with the world beyond Plymouth, and attracted a transient laboring population, informal mechanisms of accommodation and compromise were unavailing. Dispute settlement increasingly became a judicial function. Plymouth court records reveal "an enormous quantity" of litigation; the town became more litigious than any of its neighbors.[30]

Salem, another litigious town, shared common sources of discord with Plymouth. In Salem the eruption of conflict in the witchcraft trials at the end of the seventeenth century posed "the most severe challenge to confront the judicial system of Massachusetts during the entire colonial period." Salem had been founded primarily for commercial purposes. (It was, after Boston, the major commercial port in the colony.) Although communal ideals were enunciated, internal discord quickly undercut them. Indeed, Salem was criss-crossed by virtually every kind of conflict known to seventeenth-century New England towns. The Salem church was beset by division during its first decade as Antinomian and Separatist dissenters sparked religious schism. Mercantile prosperity stratified the town, and a high rate of population turnover further exacerbated instability and fragmentation.

The outlying region of the town, known as Salem Village, developed its own distinctively stable agrarian patterns. But, unable to resolve an uncertain legal and ecclesiastical status, the village was itself torn by "uncomfortable divisions and contentions."[31]

In these circumstances arbitration and church dispute settlement, common during the early years in Salem, became less trusted and more tentative. Disputes were channeled into court and arbitrators' awards were appealed. Declining church membership restricted the scope of congregational discipline. Even ministers appeared in court as plaintiffs and defendants. With private interest superseding the public weal, a Salem resident could plausibly declare that "he had no friend in Salem but the honored Court." If Salem residents could not agree, then Essex County courts might at least furnish rules for the conduct and consequences of their disagreements.[32]

It was, however, still a difficult task at the end of the seventeenth century. After a decade of intense anxiety in Salem—a consequence of annullment of the Massachusetts Bay charter, fear of Indian attacks, and a slave insurrection—the sudden agitation of young girls, who were diagnosed as witchcraft victims, activated the latent conflict. Village and town—one a traditional symbol of rural stability, the other of commercial change—were swept into the maelstrom as Salem confronted "a mortal conflict involving the very nature of the community itself." The frenzied behavior of the girls was attributed in Salem to bewitchment (while a similar outburst in Boston, at the same time, was interpreted as a religious awakening)—a crime that required legal prosecution. In a fractured community, whose very sources of legitimacy were in question, law was the only available source of authority.[33]

The Salem witchcraft trials opposed law and magic as forms of communal cohesion. A "witch" relied upon neighborly principles of sharing that newer conceptions of private property and personal privacy had all but obliterated by the 1690s. So, for example, the propriety (or legality) of milking a neighbor's cow, or crossing a neighbor's land, turned upon conceptions of private

property. The needy user, blamed for what by a legalistic definition had become an act of theft or trespass, might curse the owner
for doing the devil's work. That admonition was still taken seriously (as, indeed, it was intended), for belief in witchcraft—the
direct power of one person, by thought or word, over another
—had not entirely disappeared; it lingered as a vestigial remnant
of lapsed communal intensity. But once the Salem covenant ideal
of "watchfulness and tendernis" had subsided, neighborly inter-
dependence became burdensome and intrusive. The "witch" was
now challenging a system of private property and, implicitly, the
legal order that protected it. She (most, but not all, witches were
women) reminded townspeople of their obligations and chastised
them for reneging upon their social responsibilities. She must,
therefore, be punished by law for bewitchment; that is, for relying upon magic as a source of authority and for asserting dis-
carded norms of communal responsibility that the legal system
was not designed to protect.[34]

By the 1690s formal legal controls had largely replaced magical
beliefs. But the Salem episode demonstrated that the wrenching
transformation had not yet entirely run its course. In Salem (as
in England a century earlier), the "witches" tended to be needy,
dependent, powerless people (often servants) who had asserted
claims for benefits that the community no longer provided. They
expected benevolent supervision and neighborly intercession.
These were not, however, the attributes of bustling, commercial
Salem. So, in a powerful, tragic drama of legitimation, witches,
accusers, and prosecutors engaged in a relentless struggle to define the ultimate source of authority in Salem. Significantly, the
only witches who were executed were those who, in their de-
fiance of the court, explicitly challenged the legitimacy of legal
authority. Magic and witchcraft, obsolete forms of extra-legal
control, must be expunged by the full force of legal power.[35]
In Salem a witch's spell must no longer be availing against a
judicial verdict.

By the end of the seventeenth century communal harmony
was substantially weakened, not only in Salem but throughout

New England. In a setting that encouraged economic opportunity and religious dissent, the diminished authority of town, church, and neighbors left a vacuum for law to fill. No longer was conflict suppressed for the common weal; indeed, the meaning of the common weal was unclear. Consequently dispute-settlement procedures, once designed to turn townsmen and parishioners toward each other and inward to their community and congregation, now merely designated winners and losers among competing individuals. Arbitration and mediation had been appropriate for neighbors and parishioners, but the disagreements of strangers, who lacked any basis for mutual trust, were for lawyers and judges to resolve.[36]

Although law reigned by the eighteenth century, its rule still might waver precariously. The religious impulse, too weak to prevail, was occasionally strong enough to assert rival claims. Amid the surging revivalist zeal of the Great Awakening of the 1740s, legalism once again was criticized for circumventing morality and encouraging contentiousness. Revivalists denied the power of legal authority. Salvation, they insisted, came from God's grace, not from obedience to the cold dictates of law. The withering away of courts would lead to the good society, a society of love not law. "As for the *Business* of an *Attorney*," wrote the evangelical preacher George Whitefield, "I think it *unlawful* for a Christian, or at least *exceeding dangerous: Avoid it therefore*, and glorify God in some *other Station*."[37] But law survived the challenge, and its monopoly of civil authority increased. Indeed, a major legacy of the Great Awakening was to further strengthen the principle of dissent, which weakened the power of churches as dispute-settlement institutions and reinforced the role of secular courts. Except in isolated pockets of American society, there no longer seemed to be a viable alternative to legalized dispute settlement.[38]

During the Revolutionary era, the culmination of secular enlightenment, the older ideal of communal harmony yielded decisively to an ideology based on liberty and property. As the emphasis on individual freedom encouraged the expression of

conflict and generated the need for legal security, so the shift
from religious to secular values enabled lawyers to supersede
ministers and mediators as the primary facilitators of conflict
resolution. Joseph Hawley, a Northampton lawyer who earlier
had studied for the ministry, was admonished to "Leave the Law
to the Lawyers (few of whom enter into The Kingdom of
Heaven here or hereafter) & come over upon the Lord Side."[39]
But it was too late. Hawley's private decision was a harbinger of
social values in the new nation.

The colonial pattern of dispute settlement foreshadowed an enduring American mixture of public and private, secular and
religious, legal and non-legal. It reflected a persistent cultural
dialectic between individuals and their communities. The emergence of a pervasive legal culture, yet the persistence within it of
stubborn pockets of resistance to legalization, still expresses that
duality three centuries later.

It is tempting to see an inevitable, linear development of legal
institutions in colonial society, corresponding to the evolution,
so well known to legal scholars, from the authority of custom
to the rule of law. This would, in turn, fit snugly into the patterns of historical change that long ago became polar staples of
social theory: from primitive to modern; from status to contract;
from community to society. Each of these paired distinctions
has been used to define (and implicitly to justify) the social
changes that accompany modernization.[40] There is supporting
evidence from the colonial period for this transition: even the
substantial differences between harmonious Dedham and Sudbury
and litigious Plymouth and Salem should not disguise their common social development toward individualism, assertive contentiousness, and legalization. This process was replicated in New
York after the English conquest of New Amsterdam and, by the
early eighteenth century, even in Quaker Pennsylvania. Throughout the colonies alternative means of dispute settlement receded

amid the social and economic changes that solidified the power of legal institutions and, by the eighteenth century, encouraged the growth of a professional class of lawyers.

But if alternative dispute settlement withered, it did not disappear. Resistance to the incursions of law lingered throughout the colonial era. There were lawyers and courts, but there was a variety of alternative forums for dispute settlement which explicitly rejected legal norms and procedures. Ultimately the rule of law achieved supremacy, but law never entirely squelched its competitors. Non-legal alternatives retained their vitality, if within restricted spheres, because they continued to express a compelling vision of human relations. Disparate groups, from pious Christians to mercenary merchants, responded to their appeal.

Patterns of dispute settlement reflected the tension in colonial culture between individual and community. Although the end of the seventeenth century marked a significant divide, the lines were not frozen. Community changed, but communities remained. Individuals always asserted private rights in the tightest of communities; the subsequent encouragement of individual assertiveness never entirely obliterated communal bonds. Closed geographical enclaves may have experienced a "loss of wholeness" as common land was subdivided, religious controls were weakened, and inhabitants dispersed. But community could be a state of mind even when it no longer was a geographical place. Communal norms were retained within institutional forms that were less inclusive, but no less cohesive, than the original boundaries of church and town. Within these forms a hospitable climate for alternatives to litigation was preserved. By the eighteenth century community no longer was everywhere, but it was still somewhere. Wherever it was located, non-legal dispute settlement was likely to flourish.[41]

Merchants represented a key transitional group from colonial to modern society. Commercial arbitration is the oldest continuing form of non-legal dispute settlement in American history. As the geographical, religious, and ideological boundaries of community receded, commercial bonds were strengthened. Paradoxically, the pursuit of self-interest and profit generated its own communitarian values, which commercial arbitration expressed. The competitive individualism of the marketplace was checked by the need for continuing harmonious relations among men who did business with each other.

Commerce and community had a complex relationship. Where commercial development defined community life, as in Salem, or undercut community stability by encouraging individual acquisitiveness, as in Puritan Boston or Quaker Philadelphia, it encouraged litigation. But a pattern of commercial relationships, stitched together over time (as in New York by the end of the eighteenth century), nurtured commercial arbitration. Once commercial activity stabilized in a marketplace economy, merchants were conspicuous for their retention of anti-legal values. Their hostility to judicial dispute settlement did not recede until courts, early in the nineteenth century, moderated their own anti-commercial doctrines.[42] It may seem odd that in a highly competitive economic culture merchants and businessmen retained the most enduring commitment to non-legal dispute settlement. But though the nature of community changed after the seventeenth century, the idea of community did not disappear. Businessmen developed a community of work and profit, not of place or prayer. In a commercial society merchants were the appropriate carriers of the communitarian values of our earliest settlers.

How colonists disputed with each other depended upon how they related to each other. In communities of purpose, whether defined by ideology, ethnicity, religion, or work, they resisted formal legal institutions as harmful encumbrances. Litigation was too divisive, expensive, technical, and formal. (Nor did ministers or merchants welcome the competition of lawyers and judges for status and power.) In more randomly organized communities, however, these deficiencies were less debilitating. There law filled a social vacuum, providing a common framework of accepted procedures for mitigating conflict and resolving disputes. The source of community authority left an indelible imprint upon dispute-settlement processes. For Puritans and Quakers it was religion; for merchants, profit; but Salem endured a struggle, literally to the death, between magic and law. Yet law constituted only one among several competing systems of control in the colonies. Not until the end of the eighteenth century, when the Enlightenment sanctified the inalienable individual rights of liberty and property, was its ascendency assured. Then lawyers and courts came to monopolize dispute settlement.

Whether colonists turned away from law, or toward it, their choices expressed a coherent set of priorities. Three centuries later, however, the meaning attributed to these preferences has been altered almost beyond recognition. Where Puritans and Quakers experienced community, modern Americans would find intolerable control. Their mutual concern for each other now seems like intrusiveness; their pursuit of autonomy surely was harsh and arbitrary to outsiders. They perceived the ebb of communal impulses as disintegration, not progress. For them it encouraged isolation, not freedom.

To respond to their choices with empathy requires a willingness to suspend some basic biases of modernity. Categories that are self-evident to us were incomprehensible in the seventeenth century, when distinctions between sacred and secular, or public and private, were still unknown or unpersuasive. Community members who elevated harmony above diversity were not unduly troubled by coerced conformity. Privacy was minimal because personal affairs and private disputes were community concerns—as Mrs. Hibbens discovered. The texture of colonial life, like English village life previously and tribal culture thereafter, absorbed the best and worst attributes of communal intensity (as modern urban society so abundantly demonstrates the perils and pleasures of individual self-absorption). It is captured in the East African fable about a man who tested his neighbors, during the first night in his new village, by beating a goatskin while his wife screamed for help. There was no response, so the next day they left for another village.[43] The founders of Dedham, and the followers of Peter Noyes in Sudbury, would have understood.

Colonial society changed, but the original vision expressed in the New England town covenant never entirely vanished. As late as the beginning of the new nation in 1790, a New England town ordinance required disputes to be submitted to a committee of "three discreet freeholders." Refusal was considered to be "unfriendly to the peace of the town"; the offending disputant would be treated thereafter with "contempt and neglect."[44] By then, however, this was more the exception than the rule. Courts were numerous and accessible; a professional class of lawyers served eager litigants. To focus on the legal process because it succeeded, however, or to assume its inevitability, slights the persistence of alternatives and misses an opportunity to explore their significance. Not only did they flourish in the colonial era; they endured even after the social changes of modernization encouraged legal development. The resolution of private disputes—indeed their definition as private disputes—would henceforth occur primarily within a legal framework. But alternative forums remained available, even if the pattern of their use changed dramatically in the nineteenth century.

Chapter 2

The Divided Legacy: From Bible Communism to Industrial Commonwealth

Inspired by the religious frenzy that swept through the new nation early in the nineteenth century, Baptist preacher John Leland denounced "the host of lawyers who infest our land . . . like the swarms of locusts in Egypt, and eat up every green thing." It was to no avail. Despite persistent hostility toward lawyers among revivalists whose jeremiads rejected secular corruption for evangelical communities of the spirit, an American legal culture was securely established within a national setting. This was "the formative era," "the golden age," a crucial time of "transformation" in American law. Whether the standard of measurement is the creativity of the Marshall Court, the rapid ascent of lawyers to positions of public power, or the evolution of law as an instrument to facilitate economic growth, the expanding role of law in the young republic was evident. New England towns no longer were bound by the values of harmony and consensus. As religious dissenters, political partisans, and acquisitive merchants pursued their particular advantages, new alliances of special interest replaced older communities of common purpose. As the lines of division multiplied, the judiciary emerged as the dominant dispute-settlement institution. Even on the western frontier, which Americans have romanticized for its rambunctious lawlessness and vigilante justice, legalism seems to have been the rule rather than the exception. In the Northwest

Territory, for example, courts were quickly established, common law and statutory authority prevailed, judges followed precedent, and lawyers argued their cases according to familiar procedural rules.[1]

There still were sporadic protests against the legalization of American society. The strongest plea came from William Duane, a Philadelphian whose defense of arbitration in 1805 attracted scholarly notice more than a century and a half later. Duane compared early-nineteenth-century American society to Europe on the eve of the Reformation: law here, like religion there, had already become the mysterious monopoly of the privileged few and "none could ask *mercy of God* but through an attorney or priest." Duane wanted to end the "oppression of the people by lawyers," for litigation contributed nothing but "intolerable expense, delay, and uncertainty." Arbitration was his solution. He cited historical antecedents as far back as the Apostle Paul, including Pennsylvania Quakers, colonial merchants, recently constituted Danish conciliation tribunals, and George Washington's will (which provided for arbitration of disputes "unfettered by law or legal construction"). Duane suggested a simple legislative change, permitting either party to litigation to apply to the court for referral to binding arbitration.

Duane's faith in arbitration rested upon the conviction that justice (whose meaning was self-evident), was "the right of every man, speedily and without price." People could settle their disputes themselves, or they could represent their own interests intelligently and directly before arbitration referees. Arbitration was appropriate for "a free, enlightened, and commercial people." As Americans gained control over the dispute-resolution process they would, Duane predicted, dwell in communities where "virtue would abound. . . . The industrious and virtuous of other communities would flock to this, and none but the lazy, and vicious would quit it."[2]

Anti-lawyer feelings were sufficiently strong in the early national period to encourage state legislatures to experiment with arbitration. Massachusetts required justices of the peace to recommend it as an alternative to litigation. New York substantially expanded the scope of arbitration to encourage private dispute settlement prior to litigation. A few years after the publication of Duane's pamphlet, Pennsylvania permitted arbitration in all civil suits for less than one hundred dollars. But these experiments were short-lived; arbitration was in decline after the turn of the century. Aggressive state judiciaries scrutinized arbitration agreements more carefully and overturned them more frequently. In New York, Massachusetts, South Carolina, and even Pennsylvania, bench and bar stifled their competitors. As arbitration lapsed, even among the merchants who had been its most persistent users, non-legal forms of dispute settlement virtually disappeared. Two centuries of vigorous experimentation seemed at an end. As one historian has suggested: "a middle-class public, cherishing the ideals of competition, utilitarianism, and self-advancement, found itself unwilling to forego the advantages of an individualistic legal system in favor of some more equitable communitarian experiment."[3]

The conspicuous exceptions in the first half of the nineteenth century were the utopian communities that proliferated through New England and the Middle West. More than a hundred of these "backwoods utopias" attracted people who, for a variety of religious, cultural, and political reasons, fled the pervasive materialism and secularism of American life. Among them were New England *literati* who gathered at Brook Farm, German Lutherans who built New Harmony in Indiana, socialists attracted to the ideas of Robert Owen and Charles Fourier, and Mormon followers of Joseph Smith who made the long trek to Utah. They did what the settlers of Dedham and Sudbury had done two centuries earlier: by conscious design and common effort they created their own separate geographical and ideological communities to implement their perfectionist visions. The utopians, who sought a refuge and expressed a hope, offered a dual critique of American society. Religious utopians, many of whom belonged to dissenting Protestant sects—Shakers, Seventh Day Baptists, Swedenborgians, and assorted German separatists—despaired of secular society and constructed spiritual communities of Christian believers. Political utopians, committed to varieties of socialism, anarchism, and communism, criticized industrial society and pursued alternatives to private property, the factory system, and a competitive economy. If, from a religious perspective, society was sinful, from a political one it was unjust. An alternative social structure was required to reunite people with God, or each other, in spiritual and non-exploitive ways.

Utopians, whether religious or secular, believed in human perfectibility within a harmonious community. Their commitment required substantial sacrifices. In some communes they relinquished their private property; in others they abstained from alcoholic consumption and even sexual activity. Members lived in communal residences; ate in communal dining halls; prayed and played together; and accepted communal definitions of permissible forms of loving relationships (ranging from polygamy to celibacy). But they reaped ample rewards for their acts of renunciation. Above all, they participated in a fellowship of believers, acting in harmonious relation to their land, their God, their spiritual brothers and sisters, and their political principles.[4]

Utopian "Bible communism" challenged dominant American values. Utopians were communists in a society devoted to private property. They practiced celibacy, polygamy, community-controlled reproduction, or complex marriage (uninhibited sexual access) in a society committed to marital monogamy. They imposed communal coercion in a society that celebrated individual self-interest. And they rejected, at least in theory, the authority of the state and its system of laws, in an assertively nationalistic era distinguished by popular reverence for country and Constitution.[5] Their own source of authority—a blend of Christianity and communism—made formal legal institutions anathema. Law threatened the Christian principles of the religious communities and the socialist precepts of the political ones. Cooperative communities of believers found legitimacy in their own perfectionist objectives.

John Humphrey Noyes, the charismatic founder of the Oneida

community, asserted "the theocratic principle—. . . the right of religious inspiration to shape society" in opposition to republicanism, "the mere power of human law." Noyes had made his own personal journey from law to religion, rejecting legal study during a wave of religious revivalism in the 1830s that swept him into the ministry. "Anti-Legality" was a fundamental part of his religious and community theory. Constitutions and laws, he insisted, destroyed communal bonds by orienting members toward legal rules, not Christian precepts. Pauline teachings guided him: grace, not law, saved people from sin; it was better to suffer wrong (as the Quakers had also insisted) than to litigate. "We are very averse to litigation," Noyes wrote, "and intended . . . to preclude the possibility of it."[6]

Litigation, at Oneida and in the other Christian utopian communities, was rejected as the private equivalent of violence and war. A Shaker elder distinguished personal settlement of disputes, or the "Law of Christ," from victory through the "laws of men." Litigation represented "the final surrender of the principle of love," which was the very foundation of communal existence. The Harmony Society, as its founder Father Rapp explained, had "nither a written nor printed constitution or form of Law." Guided by Christian principles, the Society remained "pure without using constraint or rigor." In the outside world, Rapp lamented, "every thing is shaked in its base," but the Harmony Society would know nothing of such "evils & calamities."[7]

Visitors to the utopian communities frequently were impressed with the low incidence of litigation. They recorded how Aurora, a German community in Oregon, went nineteen years without resort to the courts. In the Wisconsin Phalanx, which never had a lawsuit, the use of legal counsel for dispute settlement was unknown. At Amana, in Iowa, seventeen hundred members "live in such perpetual peace that no lawyer is found in their midst." A visitor to the Harmony Society community was prompted by his experiences there to develop his own utopian proposal. To initiate litigation, he decided, would be equivalent to "an act of self-expulsion." With mutual cooperation and arbitration, but without litigation, "equity and wisdom, and not property may govern." Litigation "and other expensive evils," as an Oneida member explained, were "necessary concomitants of individual property, [which] disappear from Societies fully communistic."[8] Common ownership of property would eliminate buying and selling, interest and usury, banks and stock exchanges, competition and litigation, and—of course—judges and lawyers.

Communal order was secured through a variety of controls that were designed to eradicate conflict or to eliminate "discordant spirits." The framework for resolving disagreements was mutual and consensual, not individual and adversarial. Peer pressure was relentless, ranging from surveillance by neighbors or leaders (especially among Shakers and Mormons) to ferret out deviance, through moral suasion to guide erring members back to the community (through forms of confession and atonement), to the ultimate sanction of expulsion. As intrusive as the scrutiny seems, and surely was, members were reassured of solicitous community concern for their welfare. A staunch individualist might be appalled by the loss of privacy; a committed utopian flourished among believers who "possessed one heart and one soul and had all things in common."[9]

Yet nineteenth-century utopian communities, like their seventeenth-century predecessors, could not preserve their unity of vision no matter how strong their ideological aversion to conflict. Harmony was a persistent dream, but not a daily reality. There were mundane problems involving living or working arrangements, and more cosmic disagreements involving ideological purity or leadership authority. If surveillance did not deter deviance, and private admonition by a community leader failed, the most common mechanism for dispute resolution was some form of open meeting, which channeled conflict inward to the community and denied individuals the opportunity to pair off as adversaries. At New Harmony, dissidents and disputants were brought before an "open family assembly," which acted "unencumbered either by Creeds or Codes." At Oneida, the process was called "mutual criticism," an adaptation of Benedictine procedure that substituted communal scrutiny for formal rules. Discord was expressed openly; members (sometimes at their own initiative) were criticized by Noyes or, in extreme cases, before an assembly of the entire community. Criticism asserted the primacy of group norms over individual contentiousness. As the outside society could not exist without courts and police, Noyes wrote, "so *Communism cannot exist without free Criticism.*" Elsewhere, weekly meetings imposed a form of conflict avoidance called "non-resistance," designed to suppress disagreements by encouraging members to "smooth over any difficulty." Community arbitration was common. At Brook Farm, "all complaints, charges, and grievances" were brought to the Council of Arbiters, which offered the choice of submission or expulsion.[10]

Despite their geographical and ideological isolation, the utopian communities always existed in a social context. Total escape was impossible. Utopians might pledge to "persistently endeavor to harmonize others . . . rather than wholly rely upon [their] RIGHT," but in a rights-oriented society that was difficult. Once the bonds of community snapped, constraints on litigation vanished and "litigation between persons formerly brothers [became] a fact of life in American utopias." Ex-members asserted claims for their share of communal property; once they did, utopias were quite capable of responding, in court, with their own legalistic arguments. Often, in fact, the courts upheld them—ironically, preserving radical patterns of communal ownership with orthodox legal doctrine (usually liberty of contract) fashioned to protect private property. The utopians were too human to conceal their glee, even as sibling rivalry conquered brotherly love. "I feel quite happy," wrote Father Rapp's son, "that the validity of the articles of our Association has been tried and did stand the legal test so well."[11]

Utopian failures, like their successes, affirmed what John Humphrey Noyes already knew when he created "a little world of our own": where community ended, law began. Indeed, Noyes' Oneida provided the most poignant testimony to law as an alien value system. After three decades of remarkable harmony under

Noyes' perfectionist zeal, the community was wracked by conflict when a dissident faction challenged the charismatic basis of Noyes' authority and asserted a rival claim: the superiority of the rule of law. The trigger incident concerned the choice of Noyes' successor (Noyes preferred his son); it precipitated a major schism involving the very source of communal authority. Noyes' vision of Bible communism was challenged by James W. Towner, a lawyer and former judge whose articles and public lectures implicitly renounced charismatic authority and the rule of grace in favor of the common law, contract doctrine, and trial by jury. By 1879 Noyes, convinced by evidence of factionalism that he had lost the confidence of his community, left Oneida for Canada. Within a year Oneidans dissolved their utopia to form a joint stock company (now a successful silver manufacturing business). The Townerites subsequently departed for California, where James Towner became the first Superior Court Judge in Orange County.[12]

The Townerites, according to one of Noyes' devoted followers, wanted "a new code of morality . . . different from that you have taught." But Oneida, he insisted, "cannot be governed by law." Nor, however, could it be governed by mutual consent once the underlying source of mutuality—adherence to the principles of Bible communism under Noyes' leadership—disintegrated. Noyes understood that "confidence in me, which was the true anchor of the Community (because I was the medium of that grace which takes the place of law), sank to zero." Once it did, the rule of law could be asserted, but in utopian Oneida it could not prevail without destroying the very essence of a perfectionist community. As legal authority had squelched the magical power of witches in seventeenth-century Salem, so it overrode the charismatic authority of John Humphrey Noyes in nineteenth-century Oneida.[13]

Of all the utopians, the Mormons launched the most successful and radical venture of the nineteenth century. They built a socialist commonwealth, a virtually independent theocratic state that was self-governing, territorially autonomous, and committed to divine and Biblical inspiration (along with polygamy and, in its early years, communal property ownership). Mormon dispute settlement evolved within a community where morality, religion, and politics were fused. The Mormons were highly suspicious of "gentile" justice, which had failed to protect them against hostile mobs in Missouri and Illinois. Brigham Young described lawyers as "a stink in the nostrils of every Latter-Day Saint," and called the courtroom "a cage of unclean birds, a den and kitchen of the devil." Disputants who preferred law to Mormon justice were advised to depart for California (evidently a popular nineteenth-century den of iniquity and, therefore, an appropriate location for law-abiding Americans).[14]

Mormon internalization of dispute settlement was not only a defensive response to external hostility; it was designed to strengthen the Mormon community and preserve its principles (by punishing un-Christian conduct, for example, and by distinguishing polygamy from adultery). The Mormons combined an aversion to formal codification of their religious precepts with an elaborate ecclesiastical judicial structure to define and enforce them. Mormons, like members of other holy communities, were advised to settle disputes among themselves: "It is not right to be too technical with each other. We should . . . [use] our officials instead of resorting to the Law of the Land." In their "gospel kingdom" in the Utah desert, they developed institutions and procedures to convert disputation into harmony. The High Council president appointed church brethren as home teachers, to make monthly visits to church members to "ferret out iniquity and sin," and to resolve disagreements with arbitration. Unresolved problems were brought before a bishop's court, which could punish moral and criminal infractions (ranging from apostasy and blasphemy to cattle theft and water diversion). Final appeal was to the High Council, a body consisting of the president and two councilors, aided by twelve high priests who, in varying numbers depending upon the importance of the issue, spoke on behalf of the disputing parties. The president cast the deciding vote, in recognition of his direct access to divine revelation.[15]

At every stage of the process the overriding purpose was to preserve the unity and harmony of the Mormon community. The monthly visits of the home teachers were designed to discover or resolve (and thereby suppress) conflict before it erupted into public view. Bishop's court sessions might be held in the privacy of a church member's home, for the more private the proceedings the easier it was to maintain a public image of Mormon harmony. Wayward members constantly were prodded to rejoin the community by repenting their transgressions. In extreme situations, requiring High Council proceedings, public renunciation was demanded—again as a form of communal affirmation. An adulterer was required to "present self to people and ask for forgiveness"; a gambler was directed to "stand before people and confess wrong." Even disfellowshipping and excommunication, the ultimate sanctions, enclosed the community once again by removing its deviant members.[16]

But the Mormon experiment exceeded the limits of permissible dissent. By the second half of the nineteenth century the United States government, strengthened by the nationalistic fervor of the Civil War, had limited tolerance for flagrant challenges to dominant cultural and legal mores and for resistance to the reach of federal authority. As the weapons of war had forcibly returned the Confederacy to the Union, so the weapons of law (backed by the threat of force) tamed the Mormons. The price of peace was conformity; only when the Mormons repudiated polygamy and accepted substantial divestiture of church property did the government relent. With Mormonism reduced to a religion in a secular society, Mormon dispute settlement became a relatively minor adjunct of internal church affairs; for once Mormon society fragmented into distinct sacred and secular spheres, church sanctions lost their expansive effectiveness.

Yet even after most utopian communities had dissolved, the utopian vision lingered. Denied in actuality, it emerged as fantasy. In Edward Bellamy's *Looking Backward*, American society at the beginning of the twenty-first century has no need for lawyers because private property has been abolished. "Hair-splitting experts" have become obsolete but remain objects of curiosity for their ability "to expound the interminable complexity of the rights of property." It seems odd, in retrospect, how the American private property system once "set apart from other pursuits the cream of the intellect of every generation, in order to provide a body of pundits able to make it even vaguely intelligible to those whose fates it determined." For antiquarian interest, therefore, lawyers' treatises are preserved in twenty-first-century museums as artifacts of "intellectual subtlety devoted to subjects equally remote from the interests of modern men," who know nothing of private property.[17]

In the history of American efforts to escape from formal legal institutions, antebellum utopian communities marked the end of the beginning. The Civil War was the watershed: beyond it, amid the turbulence of race and labor relations, alternative dispute settlement was reshaped. The older pattern of indigenous community initiatives survived, but in attenuated form. Occasionally it flourished, especially in ethnic communities whose members clung to their own familiar cultural institutions amid the turmoil of resettlement in an alien environment. But in the second half of the nineteenth century, the purposes (if not the forms) of alternative dispute settlement were redefined. Fears of racial discord and class warfare injected arbitration as a remedy for the congestive breakdown of the court system and as an externally imposed deterrent to social conflict. Until the Civil War alternative dispute settlement expressed an ideology of community justice. Thereafter, as it collapsed into an argument for judicial efficiency, it became an external instrument of social control. That momentous shift still pervades the use of alternative dispute settlement more than a century later.

The first attempts to provide justice for freed slaves after the Civil War give the earliest hint of the new approach. The end of chattel slavery promised a new era of labor relations, based on contract rather than servitude, between white landowners and black field workers. But there were serious difficulties from the outset. A drastic imbalance in power relations between the races quickly converted the new labor contracts, which in theory expressed the will of freely consenting individuals, into another compulsory labor system. The Freedmen's Bureau, a government agency established to supervise and support the transition from slavery to freedom, unexpectedly confronted a huge volume of civil disputes—perhaps as many as 100,000 annually—generated by suspicion and antagonism between former masters and their newly freed slaves.[18]

General O. O. Howard, Commissioner of the Freedmen's Bureau, stumbled upon a solution. During a trip to Virginia he met with a delegation of planters who despaired of contracting with freedmen. "Cannot we blue-eyed Anglo Saxons," Howard asked, "devise some method by which we can live with him as a free man?" Spontaneously, according to his autobiographical account, Howard proposed three-man arbitration tribunals for labor-contract disputes involving less than two hundred dollars. A Bureau agent would represent the government; planters and freedmen would each choose one representative. "In nine cases out of ten," Howard blithely predicted, "the freedmen will choose an intelligent white man who always seemed to be their friend. Thus in our court so constituted, every interest will be fairly represented."[19]

This proposal expressed a paternalistic concept of fairness that rested upon continued planter domination. Howard offered arbitration to induce planters to comply with a contract labor system which already reflected and reinforced their superior bargaining position. Indeed, he seemed genuinely surprised to learn from his agents in South Carolina that freedmen there intended to choose one of their own to sit on an arbitration tribunal. When planters strenuously objected to the appointment of freedmen, Howard used his power to force their replacement. If the planters were mollified, he insisted, they would treat their black workers kindly.[20]

The internal contradictions of Howard's approach were rooted in the logic of white supremacy. Howard, like other Reconstruction reformers, believed in a blend of formal equality and paternalistic justice. Although his stated goal was equality "by law & justice," he elevated the forms of equality above its actual substance, relying upon the principle of contractual freedom despite the enormous disparity in bargaining power between whites and blacks. In this context, any substantive effectiveness of arbitration as an alternative to adjudication was undercut. Planters tolerated arbitration tribunals as long as planters controlled them. Consequently the diversion of disputes from the formal court system (where blacks, palpably disadvantaged, had no right to testify until 1866) to arbitration had few discernible benefits for the freedmen. Informality, in a social setting of disparate power relations, inevitably served the interests of the dominant group.[21]

At best, the arbitration tribunals expedited the resolution of thousands of disputes that otherwise would have thoroughly clogged southern courts. Aided by "Freedmen's courts," comprising Bureau officers and local residents, they settled small claims, wage disputes, and what Howard described as "ordinary complaints": petty theft, breaches of the peace, and disputes to which blacks were parties. The dispensation of justice in these tribunals depended upon the conceptions of equity held by the Bureau agents. They were ambivalent, pulled between their strong commitment to the freedmen and the stronger political realities of white planter domination. As a result, the effectiveness of Freedmen's Bureau tribunals varied: they might overcome the cost and delay, and occasionally even the bias, in state court proceedings. Their enforcement powers were not inconsiderable: in Mississippi and Arkansas, Bureau agents seized and sold the crops of planters who refused to abide by arbitration.[22] But their small-claims jurisdiction, and their predominantly black constituency in a society of white supremacy, limited their scope, authority, and power. With state courts reserved for southern whites, and the arbitration process itself often tilted toward planter interests, the imposition of alternative dispute settlement in the Reconstruction South ultimately expressed the values of those who administered it, not the priorities of those who were its intended beneficiaries. Blacks seldom participated as equals in either the planning or implementation of the new dispute-settlement procedures.[23]

Freedmen's Bureau arbitration exposed the vulnerability of non-legal dispute settlement without community autonomy. The freedmen, shunted from law courts to arbitration tribunals, discovered that they were powerless in both settings. If they accepted arbitration on white terms, they remained disadvantaged; if they asserted their own interests, they were usually rebuffed. Neither legality nor informality could remedy the effects of racial discrimination or economic inequality. To the contrary: as the legal system increasingly protected white supremacy (and corporate property), it ratified the disparities of power in late-nineteenth-century American society.

During the turbulent era of labor-management conflict at the end of the century, the search for a peaceful alternative to industrial violence provoked renewed interest in arbitration. Although the term "arbitration" echoed through industrial relations conferences, journals, and debates, its meaning and purpose were murky. It expressed no readily discernible community interest, nor did it elicit much enthusiasm from factory workers. The buoyant confidence that infused its earlier historical use was conspicuously absent. Instead, proponents offered arbitration as a last resort to stave off violent cataclysm in American industrial relations. Without arbitration of industrial disputes they feared the national disaster of another civil war, this time between capital and labor.

There were scattered instances of labor arbitration in the decade after the Civil War, but the sustained impetus for its adoption followed the railroad strikes and riots during the violent summer of 1877. Within the next decade a dozen states enacted legislation providing for industrial arbitration tribunals. The choices seemed clear: a "calm and intelligent" resolution of labor-management conflict or "greed and force"; "peaceful deliberations" as an alternative to "inconsiderate and fierce passions." Arbitration, lauded as "one of the simplest methods for restoring harmony where conflict exists," would extinguish the smoldering animosities left by the railroad strikes and launch a beneficent era of labor-management relations.[24]

That vision of industrial peace remained chimerical as long as employers thundered their defense of unregulated private property and their concomitant freedom to dictate terms of employment. Workers risked their jobs (and, all too frequently, their lives) if they joined a union, demanded collective bargaining, or struck in protest against intolerable working conditions. Arbitration legislation was designed to break that cycle of resistance and violence. The new laws authorized state or local tribunals, usually consisting of representatives of labor and management selected by the disputants, to arbitrate industrial grievances. There were minor variations: the disputants' representatives might be joined by a disinterested person chosen by them; or the government might appoint the arbitrators (who, in New York, came from "the two great political parties"). The arbitration tribunals, free to develop their own procedures, usually could summon witnesses and subpoena documents as any court might do. In most jurisdictions their decisions were binding upon the parties.[25]

Although the statutes proliferated, the arbitration tribunals atrophied. Disputants did not often appeal to the boards; when the tribunals appealed to the disputants they were usually rebuffed. At first, employers resisted binding arbitration as "an intolerable menace" to their property rights, which included virtually limitless power to set working conditions, to fire workers who joined unions, and to hire spies, strikebreakers, and scabs. Workers, in turn, were suspicious of a process that could serve as a strike deterrent, imposing wage rates and working conditions against their consent. Workers wanted negotiations with management, not imposed settlements. They feared that arbitration would weaken their demand for union recognition and collective bargaining. (Not an unreasonable concern, given the declaration of one Pennsylvania arbitration umpire that an owner's right to the exclusive control of his workers was of "such an unquestionable character" that interference with it was impermissible.) With workers disillusioned and employers disdainful, industrial arbitration tribunals lapsed into silence.[26]

When labor relations again erupted into violence, there was renewed interest in arbitration. Between 1886 and 1894, as the bloody carnage of the Haymarket, Homestead, and Pullman strikes revived apprehension of class warfare, worried citizens rediscovered a palliative in arbitration. After Haymarket, John Peter Altgeld, a superior court judge in Chicago (and future governor of Illinois), warned that the state, as "conservator of all classes and interests," must impose arbitration to prevent its own overthrow. Homestead was perceived as "two private armies holding a bloody carnival," a menacing regression to feudal patterns of dispute settlement. After the Pullman strike, respectable Chicagoans, shaken during "that dread hour" when "no man felt secure in his liberty, property, or possessions," gathered under the auspices of the Chicago Civic Federation to explore alternatives to industrial violence.[27]

The overriding theme of the Civic Federation conference was the impending destruction of Christian civilization (with which American society was equated) unless the hostile aggression of labor and management was tamed by arbitration. The Christian approach to labor relations required mutual respect and the willingness to engage "like men and not like brutes and savages." Arbitration, "a civilized and Christian as opposed to a barbarous and selfish" means of dispute settlement, would preserve "a Christian relation" between labor and management. Nothing less than "the highest social as well as Christian ethics" required it. The choice was arbitration or anarchy.[28]

The conference marked a significant shift in the campaign for industrial arbitration, as middle-class reformers began to assert their own interest in industrial peace more vigorously. Professors, social workers, lawyers—all fearful of social conflict—banded together and, with missionary zeal, sought to impose *their* wish for harmony upon disputants. Jane Addams pleaded for the substitution of moral suasion for physical force. For Josephine Shaw Lowell, only arbitration and conciliation expressed "a fair, a true, a noble, in one word, a Christian relation" which pointed to "mutual concession and cessation of strife." As litigation once had represented a civilized step beyond primitive combat, so arbitration marked an even higher plane of civilized relationships. With class warfare looming, the middle class assumed responsibility for softening hostility and, in the words of its worried spokespeople, for providing a framework for justice, love, honor, and faith in industrial relations.[29]

By the turn of the century the euphoric tone of Christian morality had receded, although writer Henry Demarest Lloyd, yearning for "a country without strikes," still commended arbitration for incorporating "the loftiest teachings of the loftiest apostles of the religion of humanity, the religion of labour and love." Lloyd, whose *Wealth Against Commonwealth* was an important work of late-nineteenth-century social criticism, was impressed with the level of industrial peace in New Zealand, which recently had enacted the first national compulsory arbitration statute for industrial disputes. He described arbitration tribunals as "cheap, informal, speedy courts of justice," which compelled antagonists to fight "in court according to a legal code." Although they could not alleviate the maldistribution of wealth, which Lloyd acknowledged to be the fundamental source of industrial conflict, they could civilize and, to an extent, democratize industrial relations. The appeal of arbitration, ironically, now lay in its absorption of the compulsory attributes of judicial dispute settlement. "The control of law and order," according to one proponent, would replace "the primitive method of barbaric conflict." Judicial intervention was inappropriate: either because it was biased (against workers) and belated (except when employers requested injunctions); or because marketplace bargaining did not present justiciable legal issues. But the more arbitration tribunals resembled courts, the better. Armed with the legal power to compel the participation of disputants, they would civilize labor and management with a liberal dose of legal coercion.[30]

Proponents of industrial arbitration expressed the urgency of their mission in a series of conferences during the early years of the new century. They envisioned "a friendly, undivided, and homogenous industrial commonwealth" in which labor and management cooperated to assure national prosperity. Since their interests were assumed to be identical (yesterday's worker, insisted New York businessman Oscar Straus, was today's capitalist), "why waste thought on chasms and classes?" Management representatives described industrial disputes as "merely family differences," which should be settled by arbitration within the "industrial family."[31] A rosy glow of wishful thinking suffused arbitration imagery, but the industrial family was substantially less idyllic in fact than arbitration advocates fantasized. Industrial arbitration remained a panacea offered by anxious middle-class professionals who felt dangerously squeezed between capital and labor. Their fears of impending national cataclysm prompted their fervent advocacy of arbitration as the only alternative to violent upheaval. But their pronouncements about industrial harmony encouraged employer domination (which may explain why their proposals were welcomed by businessmen who defended corporate paternalism, conservative unionism, and welfare capitalism). The vision of industrial harmony, with peaceful dispute settlement through arbitration, did not originate in the factories.

Proponents of harmony through arbitration persistently evaded the basic issues of unequal wealth and power. Employers, under public pressure to be more conciliatory, now insisted that arbitration was merely the extension of the rule of law to industrial relations. But workers still were not persuaded. Labor spokesmen resisted employer domination, even when it was expressed in benevolent family metaphors. They preferred collective action to compulsory arbitration. As one union official observed, arbitration "cannot get rid of government by injunction, abolish the monopoly of land, money, or transportation, reform the tax system, or regulate franchises of public utilities." Arbitration remained an unacceptable substitute for collective bargaining and the right to strike. If compulsory arbitration governed labor-management relations, the need for a union all but disappeared.

As long as labor remained the malnourished child of the industrial family, the arbitration process would be controlled by its domineering management parent. Compulsory arbitration, in the blunt words of American Federation of Labor president Samuel Gompers, was "industrial bondage."[32]

The rampant inequalities that pervaded labor-management relations molded the industrial arbitration process. Management owned the factories, controlled the terms of employment, and received state support in the name of law and order during times of disruption. In this setting, outside intervention usually reflected the power of the owners, not the aspirations of workers. Arbitration between unequals protected the interests of the stronger party, who could require submission and compel compliance. Even when arbitration boards encouraged a nascent form of collective bargaining (as they occasionally did during bitter labor-management disputes early in this century), the "community of interest" they promoted was fragile.[33] Workers were not comfortable with arbitration until they built strong unions within a legal framework for collective bargaining, which did not exist nationally before 1937. Until then, the vast disparity of power between labor and management, and the open warfare that punctuated American industrial relations, stifled the labor movement, which remained an unwilling and dependent participant in the arbitration process.[34]

By the beginning of the twentieth century the historical continuity of non-legal dispute settlement was seriously fractured. Antebellum efforts, concentrated within utopian communities, had extended a pattern that originated in the earliest colonial settlements in New England. The utopians understood the correlations between private property and litigation, between religious commitment and non-adversarial forms of disputation. The "backwoods utopias" were voluntary communities that depended upon the consent of their participating members (even for authoritarian leadership and rigid controls). The utopians could not always elude the reach of law, but they never imagined that its presence could do anything but inflict harm upon their purpose. After the Civil War, however, the road forked. Old sign-posts still pointed toward community autonomy and freedom from external legal controls. But down the newer path alternative dispute settlement, once a voluntary expression of communal cohesion, became an instrument of external regulation and control. No longer were its advocates participating community members; now they were outsiders, with an independent program to impose upon others. The Freedmen's Bureau relied upon informal, quasi-judicial tribunals to provide efficient access to dispute-settlement institutions for freed slaves. Advocates of industrial arbitration tried to shift disputes that were beyond the reach of legal rules to a setting where negotiation and compromise could prevail. In both instances, however, imposed harmony through arbitration preserved the status quo from which southern planters and northern industrialists derived substantial benefits. Indeed, defenders of arbitration openly identified with the dominant groups. General Howard was especially sensitive to the claims of southern planters; the National Civic Federation was attentive to the interests of northern capitalists. Arbitration, imposed upon disadvantaged victims of the racial and class conflict that divided American society, empowered its proponents more than its recipients.

Even when workers developed their own dispute-settlement institutions, they were quickly subjected to external legal controls. During the 1880s the Knights of Labor, a prominent national union dedicated to a "cooperative industrial system," established their own courts, at first merely to enforce the internal rules of their Order; then, however, as an intentional alternative to courts of law. "The workingmen are learning to despise lawyers and advocates and to eliminate law courts by establishing courts of their own," the Knights' newspaper declared. "They have long perceived that at the hands of advocates, justices and police, they get an immense amount of *law*, but no *justice*." In their courts the Knights not only punished violations of their own rules but criminal offenses (including adultery, bigamy, burglary, and embezzlement) and conduct that threatened class solidarity (most notoriously, scabbing during a strike). Theirs was, however, a fragile experiment, weakened by the steady intervention of courts of law in internal union affairs. Courts displayed "an unspoken judicial distaste for union discipline," which they limited by interpreting union constitutions as contracts that were amenable to judicial enforcement. Judicial monitoring usually was a consequence of internal union factionalism; workers who were severely disciplined or expelled (like utopian seceders) did not hesitate to appeal to the courts. Once courts intervened, however, union procedures were modified to conform to legal standards. As due-process norms prevailed, formal legal institutions drained still another source of indigenous resistance to the legal order.[35]

During the turbulence that closed the nineteenth century, legal controls served as increasingly important instruments of social cohesion. A predominantly white, secular, capitalist culture struggled to cohere amid the chaos of rapid industrialization, sharp class conflict, severe economic recession, political instability, frontier warfare, and unprecedented immigration. The rule of law provided an alternative to cultural fragmentation. As minority cultures—Mormons, workers, native Americans—were subjected to its power, their own indigenous forms of dispute settlement withered.

It is especially striking how efforts to heal the wounds of racial and class discord drew upon the historical forms, but not the historical substance, of non-legal dispute settlement. Resort to arbitration expressed the values of harmony and consensus that were associated with informality and non-legality. But in a heterogeneous, stratified culture, which encouraged aggressive, competitive individualism to maximize private gain, references to a community of mutual interest sounded increasingly hollow. The communitarian impulse still flickered: advocates of arbitration retained the memory of a community of moral order. These upright, respectable, middle-class men and women, genuinely terrified of conflict, vigorously asserted the superiority of this ideal. They also did not hesitate to impose it upon others, who might be less certain of its benefits—those for whom conflict suppression might mean external domination and control. The reformers were determined to strengthen a fragile social order —and to protect their own positions of privilege within it. Arbitration offered a fleeting possibility. But as they struggled to define a community of Christian ethics in industrial relations, the imperatives of stratification and inequality in an urban industrial society obliterated their vision. Ultimately they found greater security within the rule of law and the protective stability of a formal legal system.

Chapter 3

Law and Acculturation: Immigrant Experiences

During the early years of the twentieth century, millions of new immigrants to the United States struggled to survive in an alien, often hostile, environment. Uprooted from their native lands, they clung tenaciously to familiar remnants of their Old World cultures. They might migrate as solitary individuals, but they settled together in neighborhoods where they drew sustenance from others who not only shared the wrenching experience of their passage but the comforting memories of their traditions. Members of every immigrant group, no matter how disparate their origins, confronted a nagging dilemma: how much of their past should they shed; how American would they become? The lure of their new nation provoked fierce internal struggles which split communities, divided families, and tormented individuals. The intergenerational intensity of that dilemma resonates through modern American literature; hardly a novel or autobiography of immigrant life has spared parents and children the anguish of conflict between immigrant origins and American aspirations.

Dispute-settlement patterns absorbed these tensions. The choice to use or to avoid the American legal system touched sensitive nerves of cultural autonomy. New immigrants had good reasons to resist, at least temporarily, litigation and the judicial process. They often dwelled in communities where personal relationships were intricately social and enduring, not impersonally contractual and transitory. They did not share the prevalent American assumption that a judge, adversary relations, and Anglo-Saxon legal procedure guaranteed justice. They valued personal attributes; the status and needs of disputants were perceived as integral components of a settlement, in contrast to legal proceedings where legitimacy required assumptions of formal equality. The newcomers understood that the delicate equilibrium of continuing community relationships would be upset by the narrowing of issues, the designation of winner and loser, and the abrupt, abrasive finality of a legal verdict. Control over conflict was crucial for preserving communal values from the corrosive effects of assimilation. Alternatively, willingness to permit disputes to enter the legal system represented a long step in the journey toward absorption in American society.

The predominant geographical source of twentieth-century immigration was southern and eastern Europe, where boundaries had shifted rapidly amid the eruptions of political and economic change. As personal or political dreams were dashed into nightmares, Italians, Russians, Poles, Rumanians, Bulgarians, Slovaks, Greeks, and Armenians, desperately searching for stability and opportunity, abandoned their homes for the New World. In the United States, as in the old countries, their national identities were still tenuous; immigrant groups were internally fragmented and as divided among themselves by regional, town, and family differences as they were distinctive from each other. Beyond the mundane conflicts of daily existence were sharp religious and political disputes whose sources lay beyond the ocean in their lands of origin.[1] Yet there were also common bonds to strengthen resistance to fragmentation. Suspended between cultures, immigrants adapted or developed dispute-settlement practices that reflected this precarious duality.

In the time of insecurity that followed migration, the attraction of informal justice, combined perhaps with threats of informal vengeance, tended to divert immigrant disputes to powerful individuals who straddled their native and adopted lands. Many of the newcomers relied upon a form of the padrone system to mediate conflicting needs and expectations. The padrone, a powerful authority figure, combined various functions: primarily a labor contractor and employment broker, he was also a provider of social services and an arbitrator of disputes that immigrants were reluctant to entrust to the unfamiliar legal norms of foreigners. As arbitrator, his word carried the force of law among Italian, Greek, Turkish, and Bulgarian immigrants. They were too dependent upon him for employment, housing, and other basic needs to challenge his authority. The padrone eased the adjustment problems of his constituents as he bound them to his own power. "In a land of strangers he provided an anchor, a sense of security."[2] A traditional figure who demanded respect, he was also a transitional figure whose decisions were controlling up to a point—the point when immigrants developed the confidence to explore American channels of dispute settlement.

As the power of the padrone waned, conflict worked its way out of the immigrant enclaves into the formal legal system. Although Greek immigrants, for example, organized their own *Kinotitos*, or community governing body, it was wracked by disputes between its secular and religious members. Both factions turned to the courts to resolve disagreements over financial allocations, church property, the appropriate language for education, and the division of educational authority between church and school. In numerous Greek communities, by the World War I era, there were "lengthy court trials . . . and the extravagant use of church funds for litigation and lawyers' fees."[3]

Other immigrant groups experienced a parallel movement: away from internal, hierarchical forms of dispute settlement to the legal norms and institutions provided by American society. There was a strong pull toward the legal system. Courts and police were as important as instruments of socialization for adults as schools and teachers were for children. They inculcated social norms and expectations: obedience, respect for property and authority, and appropriate behavior toward neighbors, landlords, creditors, and employers. Most of the immigrants from southern and eastern Europe had their own reasons to feel comfortable with their transition. The more closely they conformed to the values of the dominant society the less alien they felt, and the less hostility they were likely to encounter. The majesty of the law, like the symbolism of the flag, was too alluring to resist.[4]

Among some newcomers, however, dispute-settlement practices reflected lingering resistance, rooted in Old World norms, to Western legal values. Justice without lawyers had strong appeal in the Scandinavian communities of North Dakota and Minnesota, where conciliation was part of their cultural heritage. The attempt to guide disputants toward a voluntary resolution of their difficulties, without an imposed solution or legal technicalities, dated from an eighteenth-century royal edict that promulgated conciliation as an alternative to civil litigation. A century later every Norwegian parish and village with at least twenty families still constituted a conciliation district. "Good men" served as conciliators in private proceedings from which lawyers were excluded. Courts dismissed any case in which conciliation had not been attempted.[5]

Scandinavian immigrants transported their informal procedures to the United States and, after World War I, favored legislation that implemented conciliation as an alternative to adversary relations. In 1921, the North Dakota legislature enacted the first statewide conciliation law, for controversies involving less than two hundred dollars (nearly half of all civil disputes in the state). As in Norway, no such claim could be processed in court prior to conciliation efforts. The state supreme court cited Scandinavian antecedents when it upheld the statute, noting that "every lawsuit is a miniature war." In Minnesota the impetus for conciliation was broader: it was also provoked by apprehension about judicial congestion and the need for efficient small-claims processing. It was argued that lawyers made "acquiescent" parties "litigious," so they were barred from conciliation proceedings. Law reformers added their elitist support for conciliation: they expected disputants from "the more ignorant classes" (located largely among the urban poor) to defer to the conciliator, identified as a "trusted public officer" who would guide them to an agreement.[6]

The most tenacious defense of traditional practices came from Chinese and Jewish immigrants. Despite their evident cultural differences, they shared certain attributes which differentiated them from the overwhelming majority of voluntary immigrants to the United States. Both were, of course, outsiders to Western Christianity; indeed, both had been deeply wounded by it. Anglo-Saxon legal institutions not only were foreign, but often overtly hostile. Chinese and Jewish newcomers, fiercely determined to preserve distinctive cultural identities, retained institutions of conflict resolution that antedated Anglo-American common-law courts by centuries.

Chinese mediation and Jewish arbitration were the most enduring forms of indigenous immigrant dispute settlement. The Chinese experiment was enclosed within Chinatowns and has remained largely inaccessible to Western outsiders. But it provides fragmentary evidence of sustained resistance to acculturation while the Chinese preserved an insulated enclave within American society. Jewish arbitration, by contrast, suggests the complexities of immigrant dispute settlement not only as a form of cultural resistance but as a process of cultural adaptation. Accommodation, after all, was an integral part of Jewish history and a pervasive theme of the American Jewish experience.

According to a Chinese proverb, "It is better to be vexed to death than to bring a lawsuit." Confucian culture valued harmony within a communal setting. The assertion of rights not only was disruptive; it dangerously elevated the individual above his family, clan, or village. For centuries, mediation by family elders and village headmen functioned to restore intricate and delicate patterns of personal relations to their proper equilibrium. As fathers resolved family disputes, so headmen, selected by villagers, mediated disputes among neighbors. Direct approach to a public official was rare and elicited a severe reprimand from village elders. The mediation process reminded disputants that group norms, asserted by the elders, provided the only acceptable framework for the resolution of differences.[7]

The preservation of harmony exacted its price: the enhanced power of mediators and reinforcement of the social structure that sustained their position. Educated, powerful, and wealthy Chinese elders used their leverage to strengthen their rule within a hierarchical, deferential social order. Although mediation, in that setting, might be a subtle, sophisticated form of coercion, litigation was perceived as an infinitely less satisfactory alternative. Not only was litigation expensive, time-consuming, and unpredictable, it disrupted harmony and represented a degrading confession of personal failure. Resort to law assured bitter relations between disputants and their clan members or neighbors. "Once go to law," according to a Chinese admonition, "and there is nothing but trouble."[8]

Chinese immigrants to the United States transplanted their strong aversion to legal forms of dispute settlement. Their preference for mediation was strengthened by the overt bias of American judicial institutions. Especially in California, where the first wave of Chinese immigrants settled, their primary experience with courts was as defendants or victims. During the 1850s the California Supreme Court ruled that the testimony of Chinese witnesses against whites was inadmissible, pronouncing the Chinese "a race of people whom nature has marked as inferior." The blatant hostility of the American legal system, combined with its foreign procedures and language, provided a strong incentive to retain internal mediation as the primary method of dispute settlement. Additional reinforcement probably came from the original intention of the Chinese to be no more than temporary sojourners in the United States.[9]

American Chinatowns were conspicuously insular, reflecting both cultural pride and the insecurity of relocation amid hostile foreigners. But their mysterious distinctiveness—so menacing and inscrutable to outsiders—masked persistent internal disruptions. During the last half of the nineteenth century, San Francisco's Chinatown was wracked by violent conflict between feuding clans, secret tongs, and challengers to merchant authority. Chinese-Americans seemed bound together, if at all, by "antagonistic cooperation." Facing the constant danger of fragmentation, they searched for sources of cohesion.[10]

Chinese immigration involved the transfer of loyalties from native clans and villages to their representatives in the United States. A transplanted form of "headman adjustment," exercised through the local benevolent associations, mediated conflict in American Chinatowns as it did in Chinese villages. In the United States, merchants dominated the associations and comprised a "benevolently despotic" ruling elite. Their wealth, translated into power, enabled them to serve as intermediaries between the impoverished, indentured immigrants and American society. As contractors and brokers, they provided jobs, favors, protection, and punishment. The merchant elders also were dispute mediators. They acted within a hierarchical community structure of clan and local associations, with the Chinese Consolidated Benevolent Association, an umbrella council that resolved disputes between clan or district factions, at the pinnacle. At every level, the merchants struggled to contain conflict within tolerable bounds and to impose sufficient control to mitigate the danger of divisive factionalism. According to one observer, "Woe unto a Chinese who does not abide by the rulings of these associations, for he is marked as a suspicious person and an outlaw." Ostracism, mixed with shame of public scrutiny (and, no doubt, an occasional threat), was a strong deterrent; appeal to the civil courts was extremely rare (although, in one instance, a madam prosecuted extortionists who overtaxed her brothel.)[11]

Once the Chinese settlers made a permanent commitment to the United States, by the end of the nineteenth century, traditional constraints against litigation began to crumble. Mediation and adjudication became weapons in a struggle for community control and for freedom from community boundaries. As the liberating aspects of American culture weakened older controls, courts could serve the needs of those who pursued freedom. Indentured workers, for example, took merchants to court in efforts to escape rigid creditor contracts and high interest rates. But the merchants (with the assistance of lawyers) succeeded in removing these complaints from court dockets, returning them to mediation and to the jurisdiction of the benevolent associations. Their own community control system, resting on loyalty, filial piety, and fear, depended in part upon their ability to contain disagreements within Chinese dispute-settlement institutions.[12]

For several generations, traditional mediation flourished in American Chinatowns. Not until after World War II did its power show serious signs of attrition, as an American-born Chinese population, with its own distinctive set of values, grew restive within the old constraints. The traditional leadership was discredited by its failure to resolve pressing social problems (poverty, racism, unemployment, inadequate housing) in the community. The elders clung to their role as mediators, but as their power base was undercut disputes flowed more readily into lawyers' offices and judges' chambers. Mediation no longer was needed to soothe frightened immigrants in an alien environment, nor could it protect elite control once traditional authority collapsed.[13]

Among the various immigrant groups for whom internal dispute-settlement procedures were vital for community cohesion, none migrated with as strong a historical commitment to law, and as deep a mistrust of alien legal systems, as the Jews of Eastern Europe. Jews were a people whose religion was law; they clung to the Torah to preserve their identity as a people during two millenia in dispersion, while they were suspended in exile, at least spiritually, between their temporary residence and their once and future home. (In the most literal respects, the Torah was their living law: Jews danced with their holy scrolls in celebration; the Torah, if profaned, was buried in a cemetery.) Yet necessity constantly imposed the burden of adaptation. As Jews were reminded all too frequently and tragically, they dwelled in other nations at the sufferance of their Gentile hosts. Reverence for their own law always involved sufficient flexibility to permit survival in the threatening environment of Jewish dispersion.

According to Talmudic doctrine, the law of the state was the law that governed Jews. This principle of accommodation co-existed uneasily with the autonomy necessary for Judaism to endure; conflict between Jewish law and the law of the state was inevitable. (Indeed, it was doubtless such conflict that had generated the Talmudic principle.) Jews had struggled with this problem at least as far back as the second century, when the Romans abolished Jewish courts and Jews developed their own informal dispute-settlement procedures as an alternative to litigation in Roman tribunals. Disputants selected their own arbitrators; communal pressure encouraged compliance with their decisions. By the Middle Ages Jews had centuries-old admonitions against bringing their disputes before "heathens," even if a non-Jewish court would have decided a case consistently with Jewish principles. According to Maimonides, Jews who submitted disputes to Gentile judges "cause the walls of the Law to fall." Jews who resorted to Christian courts might be treated as informers, guilty of treason against divine and Mosaic law. External hostility reinforced internal constraints. Often Jews were not permitted to testify in court; special oaths were required of them when the plaintiff or defendant was Christian.[14]

The retention of disputes within the Jewish community was not merely a defensive response to external hostility. It expressed deep desires for religious and cultural autonomy in exile. To sustain their distinctiveness as a people within a state, Jews relied upon the synagogue, their house of prayer, and the Bet Din, their house of judgment. The Bet Din, or rabbinical court, was in theory restricted to religious issues. But in practice, Judaism made no clear demarcation between religious and secular spheres. By the Middle Ages, only serious crimes involving capital punishment were explicitly beyond Bet Din jurisdiction. Disputes were judged by rabbis, before whom parties pleaded without the assistance of counsel. (Lawyers were feared for their ability to manipulate and distort, and especially for their willingness to rely upon the law of the state, instead of Jewish law, when state law might better serve their client.) Amid procedural informality

there was considerable substantive formality: decisions were based
not only upon written Jewish law but upon the known precedents
of other Jewish courts. In virtually all religious and civil matters,
including family and commercial disputes, the decisions of the
Bet Din were binding. But Bet Din legalism was softened by
other considerations. Justice required reconciliation, not victory.
According to Maimonides, "a court which always settles cases
by *pesharah* [compromise] is praiseworthy."[15] So the Bet Din
combined the forms and substance of law with the informalities
of community arbitration. It provided an internal, legalistic alternative to Christian regulation of Jewish affairs.

The complexities for Jews of a dual legal system were intensified in the nineteenth century by the Enlightenment and
emancipation. Jews were promised legal equality and citizenship;
in return, they were expected to compress Judaism into a religion.
As the traditional wholeness of Jewish life was sharply bifurcated
into sacred and secular spheres, the jurisdictional role of Jewish
courts was reduced. Milder penalties were now imposed for
diverting disputes from Jewish courts, suggesting that such de-
fections were more frequent. Offenders were still punished with
banishment from the community, but their removal was more
symbolic (exclusion from Torah readings) than actual (excommunication). The authority of the Bet Din was confined to "religious" questions—in the modern world the questions that held
the least significance for the most people.[16]

The mass exodus of Eastern European Jewry around the turn
of the twentieth century further devastated Jewish community
life. Institutions already weakened by more than a century of
turbulent change in Europe were not easily transplanted to
America, especially when the most secular Jews displayed the
greatest eagerness for the opportunities emigration afforded.
They, of course, were the uneasiest carriers of tradition. Breaking
with the past, they confronted the peril and the challenge of
building new lives and new communities in their adopted land.
But the centrality of law in Jewish history was, with intriguing
variations, replicated in the American Jewish experience.

American Jews transformed old institutions into forms appropriate to their new setting. The difficulties of the task were compounded by the suspicious encounter of sharply clashing Jewish cultures, especially in New York, the center of American Jewish life. Established German Jews viewed the ragged, impoverished newcomers with a mixture of sympathy, condescension, and disdain. The immigrants responded with respect, mistrust, and apprehension. They needed assistance, which German Jewish philanthropists and social workers provided. But the price was high: immigrants were expected to Americanize rapidly lest their conspicuous poverty and distinctive manners cast aspersions upon even the most assimilated German Jews, who worried that their own successful absorption and comfortable status were in jeopardy.[17]

The search for coherence and order within a communal framework prompted the revival of a venerable European institution, the *Kehillah* (Hebrew for "community"), to coordinate communal activities and, if possible, to speak for New York Jewry with a single voice. The *Kehillah*, an inclusive organization designed to represent the interests of New York Jews, forged a tenuous alliance among socialists and Zionists, assimilated German-Americans and Yiddish-speaking newcomers, philanthropists and factory workers, Reform and Orthodox rabbis. For religious and secular reasons, dispute settlement figured prominently in *Kehillah* activities. The dispute-settlement functions of rabbis were virtually moribund in the United States. The rabbinate was in disarray, ripped from its Old World foundation. *Kehillah* leader Judah L. Magnes developed a plan for neighborhood rabbinical judges to answer questions of ritual and to mediate minor disputes. Their participation in dispute settlement was intended to restore a traditional rabbinical function, but it could not restore the rabbinate to its traditional place in the Jewish community. The rabbis resolved a restricted sphere of ritual issues for a dwindling constituency.[18]

For the overwhelming majority of immigrants, earning a living was more urgent than ritual purity. In the teeming commercial world of the Lower East Side, labor-management conflict, spiced by European socialism and militant feminism, cleaved the community. A series of strikes in the clothing industry during 1909–10 stirred forebodings of class warfare in the absence of a conciliatory framework. Julius Henry Cohen, counsel to the manufacturers (and subsequently a prominent advocate of commercial arbitration), cited the European Jewish experience as a model for successful dispute settlement through mediation. In response, the *Kehillah* established a Bureau of Industry, staffed by full-time mediators, whose efforts in the clothing, fur, and millinery industries brought a measure of harmony to industrial relations in the sweatshops and factories where Jewish immigrants worked.[19]

Kehillah leaders then looked beyond industrial mediation to a more inclusive pattern of dispute settlement for the full range of conflict in the Lower East Side. An experiment in Baltimore sparked their interest. There Jewish lawyers, distressed by corrupt justices of the peace, had established a lay arbitration tribunal for the resolution of commercial (and also religious) disputes among Jews. But New York law, which encouraged the easy revocation of arbitration agreements, was an impediment. While Magnes lobbied diligently (and successfully) for legislative reform, his associates developed a plan for *Kehillah* arbitration. By 1914 a Court of Arbitration and a network of neighborhood arbitration boards functioned within the Jewish community of New York.[20]

The theme of harmony resounded through *Kehillah* arbitration literature. Community leaders, concerned with the intensity and potential disruptiveness of conflict among their own constituents, looked to arbitration to restore "peaceful relationships" among friends and neighbors. There was, additionally, a defensive side to *Kehillah* arbitration, consistent with the traditional Jewish preference not to display dirty linen before a hostile Christian public. Squabbles must be contained within the community lest outsiders suspect division and weakness, or draw unsavory conclusions that might fuel anti-Semitism. Disagreements between Jews were regarded by arbitration proponents as "family dif-

ferences . . . in which the public is not interested." Public attention, according to a *Kehillah* executive committee member,
"would be unfortunate and militate against the good name of the
Jewish community." If a dispute went to court one party would
win, but "the Jews as a body" surely would "suffer much more
in reputation."[21]

The arbitration tribunals straddled the secular and religious
worlds, blended informality and legality in their composition and
procedures, and spoke in the various tongues of their constituency. (The official language was English, but opinions were also
announced in Yiddish, the language of the Lower East Side. The
contrast with Chinese tribunals is instructive: Chinese immigrants,
intending to return to China, retained their native language.)
In disputes over ritual issues that were enforceable by "religious
or moral suasion" the parties were urged to select a rabbi as arbitrator; his decisions were expected to be "as free as possible" from
"the strict rules of technical legal evidence." (In at least one
Kehillah district, a Bet Din functioned in conjunction with the
local arbitration court to provide disputants with their choice of
forum.) When rabbis were not conspicuous, lawyers were. Legal
representation of the parties was prohibited, but lawyers usually
sifted the complaints, dismissed those without merit, advised the
parties, and guided the selection of arbitrators.[22] Gradually community power drifted from the rabbinate, and dispute settlement
began to function as an instrument of immigrant acculturation
rather than as a shield to protect religious isolation.

The *Kehillah* faded away after World War I, its fragile cohesion shattered by the fractiousness of New York Jewry and its
concerns overwhelmed by a new agenda of international issues
relating to Zionism and statehood. But there was still a compelling
need to preserve Jewish religious and communal values. During
the war, the Jewish Ministers' Association of America was organized to unite Orthodox congregations against "flagrant desecration
of the Sabbath," the "ruined Jewish home," and the "lamentable
state of Jewish education." Among its contributions was a Jewish
arbitration court, designed to provide "Jewish justice" and to

preserve Jewish values against secular erosion. The arbitration principle expressed a "more modest" communal vision than the *Kehillah* had pursued, but it lingered long after the *Kehillah* had expired.[23]

In the post-war decade the New York Jewish community generated a variety of arbitration tribunals whose presiding rabbis, despite divergent religious persuasions, shared a common vision of acculturation. Samuel Buchler, an Orthodox member of the Ministers' Association, described his arbitration court as "a medium of assimilation into cosmopolitan life." It did not, he emphasized, contribute "to isolation from the life of the citizenry. On the contrary, it has served to enhance appreciation of the nature of religious liberty, and encourage respect for the authority of the civil courts." Similarly, Israel Goldstein, a prominent New York Conservative rabbi, defended his Jewish Conciliation Court for its vital role "in the Americanization process of many Jewish immigrant families."[24] Americanization required a delicate balance between secular and religious interests and between Jewish and American values. So the tribunals invariably included a rabbi, a lawyer, and a layman (usually a businessman). The rabbi symbolized continuity with religious tradition; the lawyer offered reassurance that the law of the state would not be contravened; the businessman provided access to the practical values of commerce. Like carefully balanced political tickets, the post-war arbitration tribunals stitched together the various constituencies of the New York Jewish community.

The range of disputes that came to these tribunals was as varied as the tribulations of their Jewish working-class clientele: a disgruntled widow refused to pay the rabbi for his uninspired eulogy; a disenchanted spouse felt cheated by the marriage-broker's assurance of an "everlasting" marriage; an observant husband and his assimilated wife disagreed over the retention of a *mezzuzah* on their door-post after they moved from the Lower East Side to a more respectable address (the woman was apprehensive lest the religious object cost her daughters prospective secular suitors). The arbitration process was always casual, inhibited neither by procedure nor by precedent. The parties agreed to be bound by the arbitrators' decision. (Occasionally challenged, it was invariably affirmed by the state supreme court.) No matter how bitter the disagreement, the choice of arbitration reflected a preference for dispute resolution within the framework provided by Jewish values and Yiddish immigrant culture.[25]

Nevertheless, the pursuit of Jewish justice was occasionally elusive among the discordant babble of Jewish voices. The competing claims of traditional Judaism and American modernity, of elite control and popular preference, were difficult to reconcile, and the various tribunals had their own conflicts involving power, respectability, and status. These quarrels suggest that protecting the reputation of the Jewish community, their ostensible common purpose, was uncommonly difficult at a time of wrenching transition from the Old World to the New.

The Jewish Arbitration Court, launched under Orthodox auspices by lawyer-rabbi Samuel Buchler, secured a base of philanthropic and professional support during the twenties. It resolved thousands of disputes, and was sufficiently active to justify the establishment of branch offices in scattered Jewish neighborhoods throughout the city. There is a hint, however, that lawyers who organized the court (nobly dedicated to the pursuit of "Truth, Law and Peace") may have capitalized upon its more lucrative disputes to enrich their private practices. By the end of the decade, the avid pursuit of clients, especially by immigrant lawyers, was viewed unkindly by the legal establishment in New York. A publicized investigation of "ambulance-chasing" produced a spate of disbarments and considerable righteous condemnation (especially from lawyers whose family connections, law-firm partnerships, and social clubs provided more discreet advertisements for themselves). The Arbitration Court, evidently unsettled by these developments, invited Israel Goldstein, a young rabbi from one of the oldest Conservative congregations in New York, to repair the damage to its reputation. Within a year, however, a new tribunal emerged; the Jewish Conciliation Court of America was incorporated "to advance the cause of the amicable adjustment of disputes . . . affecting the good name and reputation of Jewry."[26]

Goldstein had a shrewd understanding of the politics of institutional success, a firm conception of Jewish honor to protect, and extensive contacts among prominent Jews whose vision of purpose (and power) he shared. He obtained their support for the efforts of the Conciliation Court to preserve harmony, achieve respectability, and prod immigrants along the road to Americanization.[27] The court, like other Jewish philanthropic and social-service ventures, combined some of the strongest desires and deepest anxieties of American Jews, who were apprehensive lest the tide of Eastern European Jewish immigrants obliterate their own precarious beachhead of decorum and success. They wanted to Americanize the newcomers by scrubbing away their orthodoxy and *Yiddishkeit* with Reform, patriotism, and the King's English. Dispute settlement (removed from Bet Din orthodoxy but not yet consigned to the scrutiny of Christian judges) moderated intratribal Jewish conflict and cleansed it for public scrutiny.

Jews who brought their disputes to the Conciliation Court were, in Goldstein's words, "my humble, often underprivileged brothers and sisters, who were in need of help, sympathetic understanding, and guidance." Resolving their disagreements was the primary task of the court, but not its exclusive purpose. The preservation of Jewish dignity and honor depended upon the resolution of conflict between Jews by Jews. Not only was it unreasonable to expect Christian judges to penetrate the intricacies of Jewish ritual or custom; it was dangerous to give them the opportunity. (Occasionally, a state court judge perceived his own disability: in one dispute involving conflict between a congregation and a school over possession of a Torah the judge told the parties, "You have come to Rome. I will show you the way to Jerusalem," and referred them to Jewish arbitration).[28] Once a dispute entered the public domain it might desecrate the Jewish name and invite anti-Semitic retribution. Unassimilated immigrants must be protected from the hostility that their Old World manners and mores would elicit.

The pursuit of dignity was complicated and frustrated, however, by the tormenting persistence of Rabbi Buchler's Arbitration Court. The Buchler court (perhaps too Orthodox and obtrusive for its Conservative rival) was treated like a nagging Old World uncle, whose mere presence (to say nothing of his uncouth behavior) constantly embarrassed assimilated family members. They were still sufficiently insecure in their new home to worry constantly about what the neighbors might think of them, especially for having such an offensive relative. Goldstein invested Buchler and his court with enormous power to inflict harm on the Jewish community, which only magnified the responsibility of Goldstein's court to preserve the good name of Jewry.[29]

The bad feelings between the tribunals surfaced when the Arbitration Court began to broadcast its proceedings. The practice infuriated Goldstein and his associates, who denounced it as a degradation of Jewish honor. "Radio courts," they insisted, were nothing but "cheap sensationalism," exposing conflict merely for audience amusement. But the allegations (even if true) missed an important point: radio broadcasts invited the Jewish masses to participate vicariously in a compelling drama of conflict and catharsis. The radio, a new medium of direct communication, instantly transformed an individual dispute into a communal concern, thereby stimulating communal participation in the disputing process.[30] The Conciliation Court, which tried to stifle the broadcasts, was itself a competitor in the marketplace of disputes. As one official posed the dilemma: "While we must be both proper and dignified, we must, in some way, overcome the competition" from rival courts. Thus, the Conciliation Court cultivated good relations with the Jewish and secular press; it encouraged the *Forward*, the popular Yiddish newspaper, to cover its proceedings; and its definition of propriety permitted news-

paper advertisements. (But the printed word was carefully moni-
tored: in an early decision about publicity pamphlets Goldstein
rejected "Semitic" typeface for a more dignified alternative.)[31]

The tribunals, as voluntary institutions that depended upon
disputes for their survival, competed vigorously for a share of
the Jewish audience. Some spoke from the Lower East Side (the
Jewish Board for Justice and Peace, conducted by a radio station,
was located adjacent to a Loew's theater to capture departing
movie-goers in search of more entertainment). Goldstein's Conciliation Court, reflecting his elitist preferences, prodded disputants to be good Jews, and to become good Americans. To do
this, he relied upon "the very best element in this community . . .
a selective gathering." Not only as donors but as judges, their participation was vital to the acculturation process. Among the
leaders of New York Jewry, they provided a model of respectability and decorum for disputants. The Conciliation Court convened its sessions on the Lower East Side, but its judges traveled
to East Broadway from the Upper West Side, where the "best"
Jews lived. It was a short subway ride, but it represented a
journey of cultural refinement that usually took at least a generation to achieve. The Conciliation Court proudly touted its roster,
which included philanthropist Jacob R. Schiff, David Sarnoff of
RCA, and a cross-section of prominent judges, rabbis, and lawyers.
But between these successful acculturated Jews and the struggling
new immigrants whose disputes they resolved (the relation was
never reversed) existed a cultural gap as wide as the ocean that
separated Europe from America.[32]

If shared communal experience was the measure of empathy,
however, there were deficiencies in the principle of selection.
One self-critical judge wondered whether three imported listeners,
hearing a dispute without any specialized knowledge or prepara-
tion, could render qualified judgment. Once, when Goldstein
tried to arrange interesting sessions for favored English visitors
to preside over, he had to be cautioned to seat them on the same
panel with Americans, who would be more familiar with the

culture of the disputants. And the occasional trading of a judge-ship for a donation, to secure necessary income, hardly strength-ened the process of dispute settlement. In the end, the beneficiaries of that process were not only the disputants but the dispute resolvers, whose good name was protected as they spread their influence in the Jewish community. A photograph taken in 1954 provides vivid testimony of the distance between judges and judged: arrayed behind Supreme Court Justice William O. Doug-las, speaking at the twenty-fifth anniversary celebration of Gold-stein's presidency, are well-dressed, clean-shaven men (and one trim woman) identified as guests of honor by their various titles —Doctor, Judge, General. Closest to the camera is an elderly couple, identified merely as "two clients." The full-bearded man wears a black hat that signals his religious orthodoxy; the woman wears a baboushka, a loose-fitting peasant dress, and a shawl. They are evidently uncomfortable; unlike the other guests, their eyes are carefully averted—from both speaker and camera.[33] In the Conciliation Court, the Jews of modernity sat in judgment upon the Jews of tradition.

For the Jewish Conciliation Court, the final stage in its own acculturation process, appropriately, involved a name change. In 1939, in a modest alteration of symbolic significance, the court became the Jewish Conciliation Board. The change had been suggested two years earlier by a lawyer who anticipated state legislation prohibiting any private group from using "court" in its title. Goldstein, supported by the board of directors, had resisted the proposal as an implied demotion that would diminish the stature of his court. But the proliferation of ethnic and re-ligious tribunals remained troublesome to bench and bar, who wanted to protect the legitimacy of courts by confining the name to government institutions. Renewed pressure from established Jewish lawyers was brought on the Conciliation Court to con-sult with "the right people"—prominent Jewish judges and bar leaders—and reach "a correct conclusion." The executive secre-tary was instantly persuaded: "We should have the complete approval of the Judiciary and the Bar Associations and if by changing our name we would have such approval, we ought to do so." Goldstein and the directors concurred.[34]

The name change symbolized a subtle shift in the court's evolving identity. At first, Goldstein had resisted the change as an affront to the Jewish community it served; then he acceded to retain the approval of bench and bar, an entirely different constituency. The word of lawyers was now the law. As the Conciliation Court became the Jewish Conciliation Board, its transformation into an American institution was complete. The first step had been the decisive rejection of Rabbi Buchler's court as an embarrassing symbol of parochial orthodoxy. Then came the imposition of propriety, decorum, and honor as primary norms of acculturation, encouraging the immigrants to adjust to their American environment. The name change was the final gesture: under pressure from the formal legal system the court proclaimed its American identity.

Despite immense pressure for acculturation, remnants of the immigrant culture survived. Elderly Jews, enclosed in tradition, remained isolated from the dominant patterns of American society. Decades after the era of mass immigration had ended, and long after their upwardly mobile children had departed for the suburbs (where there were no Jewish courts), their preference for "Jewish justice" over law reflected not only their continuing marginal status in America but the strength of their bonds to the Old World culture that they had never entirely abandoned. Jewish tribunals still provided a reassuring framework. Whether it was the substantive principles that guided a decision, the presence of a rabbi (and the exclusion of Christians), or the neighborhood proximity of the proceedings and the comforting knowledge that Yiddish could be spoken there, disputants who selected that forum still preferred to insulate their Jewishness from American society.

In recent years, heightened feelings of pride among younger Jews have even spurred renewed interest in rabbinical courts as an arbitration model deserving of revival. The historic function of the Bet Din—to preserve Jewish communal autonomy and to resist the incursions of an alien culture—was sympathetically reconsidered during the 1970s, as American society fragmented into an uneasy blend of tribal loyalties and rampant individualism. The notion of an organic Jewish community, deriving legitimacy from the consent of its members, was a consistent theme in the literature of rediscovery. The Bet Din would try "to re-align and reorder" disrupted relationships, not designate winners and losers. Parties could participate actively in the resolution of their own disputes, strengthening the process of community decision-making within a framework of traditional Jewish values.[35]

For most American Jews, however, emigration and acculturation decisively rearranged their commitment to law. As Jews capitalized upon their unprecedented opportunities in the United States they developed a boundless love affair with American law. Traditionally, religious law had preserved the Jewish community; in the United States, secular law provided an escape from it. Jews arrived in America with important middle-class values already internalized, at a propitious historical moment of rapid urbanization, industrialization, and professionalization. They capitalized upon their opportunities to rise rapidly in occupational status and affluence. The legal profession attracted droves of ambitious Jews who thirsted for personal fulfillment. Law, like medicine and education, drew them in numbers vastly disproportionate to their distribution in the national population. Jews had an abiding faith in law as their only reliable safeguard against the reversions to violence that had victimized them throughout their history. By the second generation (occasionally in the first), they were far along the professional road from rags to robes, from shyster to Wall Street—and even to the Supreme Court.[36]

As the children of immigrant Jewish parents entered the legal profession they pledged allegiance to the rule of law. That strident celebration of law was most evident in the lives and careers of Felix Frankfurter and Alexander M. Bickel (but equally present in numerous less prominent lawyers). The United States was their adopted land; law was their civil faith. Both men were

European Jewish immigrants who, a generation apart, made the symbolically decisive journey from the ghetto, moving from City College in New York—the first step for ambitious Jewish boys —to the Harvard Law School. Each was a passionate advocate of the liberal social causes of his day: Frankfurter actively in the Sacco-Vanzetti case and Bickel more distantly in his *New Republic* essays (written between 1956 and 1974, touching major social issues from civil rights to Watergate). Yet Frankfurter as a Supreme Court justice, and Bickel as a constitutional scholar at Yale, staunchly defended judicial restraint and the morality of legal procedure over competing moral imperatives (Is the law good? Is the procedure fair? Is the cause just?) long after their legalistic principles had become staples of political conservatism. One senses in each of them strong ambivalence between justice and law, between moral independence and political safety, with the balance finally tilting decisively toward the stability of law. Their unabashed reverence for legal symbols doubtless afforded security (for themselves as American Jews) amid the menacing turbulence that may all too often have reminded them of what they had left behind in Europe.

Frankfurter had struggled during much of his early life to repudiate "his father and his face"—his immigrant Jewish origins —by cultivating the approval of Brahmin culture. He adopted Oliver Wendell Holmes, Jr., and Franklin D. Roosevelt as his gods, worshipping at the altars of law and patriotism. Although Frankfurter was deeply sensitive to questions of minority status and religious freedom, he invariably disclaimed personal involvement whenever these issues came before the Supreme Court. As a jurist, he gave priority to prevailing standards of constitutional orthodoxy, which prescribed judicial deference to the legislative will—even when the legislature enacted a compulsory flag-salute statute over the First Amendment objections of religious minorities. Law was his religion; the flag was his most revered symbol.[37]

For Bickel, the sixties provided disturbing reminders of impending cataclysm. The more precarious American society seemed, and the more disobedient its younger members, the more he retreated from earlier assertions of broad moral principles (especially the moral rightness of desegregation) to a "political philosophy of procedure." Edmund Burke, the eighteenth-century conservative, became his most frequently cited authority. The distance Bickel traveled in his journey to legalism can be calculated in even more personal terms. The Bickel family tradition, conspicuous by its diminishing Jewish intensity, had been lovingly presented by Bickel's father (a lawyer in Europe who became a Yiddish writer in America). "What security can there be," Shlomo Bickel asked plaintively, shortly before he died, "for one like me, who had in common with my generation cast off the burden of *Mitzvot* [commandments]?" Only fidelity to the commandments of Jewish law, he concluded, "can give a Jew a little Jewish freedom in the Freedom of the Emancipation." But the son, nearing the end of his own life, wrote: "the highest morality almost always is the morality of process."[38] The security of the rule of law, with its emphasis upon procedure and technicality, was his answer to his father's question.

Appropriately enough for the late sixties, all these issues descended to the level of parody in the courtroom of Judge Julius Hoffman, the assimilated, conservative German Jew who presided over the trial of the Chicago Eight for inciting riots during the tumultuous Democratic Party convention of 1968. Hoffman jousted repeatedly and furiously with Jewish defendants whose provocations threatened the decorum of law and order that the judge struggled desperately to maintain. He raged at a Jewish defense witness for wearing a *kepa* (religious skullcap), insisting upon its removal. (The witness, claiming religious observance, refused; at the prosecutor's request, Judge Hoffman finally relented.) The judge battled with his namesake, defendant Abbie Hoffman, over issues of decorum, order, and respect, in what one commentator aptly interpreted as "an intra-Jewish fight, a play within a play, as the two Hoffmans acted out an ancient scenario: the socially unassimilated Eastern European Jew versus the assimilated German Jew who 'passes' among the *goyim*." The more the judge wrapped himself in the American flag and defended the majesty of law and the necessity of decorum, the more he was tormented with reminders that he was, beneath it all, a Jew. Indeed, Abbie Hoffman berated him as a Jew who had become *Shande fur de Goyim* (which, in Abbie's loose translation, meant "front man for the WASP power elite").[39]

But the underlying issue was deadly serious. The judge was being challenged to rearrange his priorities: to become more of a Jew. It seemed inconceivable to Abbie Hoffman that a Jew would defend the legal symbols of an alien culture. The judge, Abbie implicitly insisted, must relinquish his commitment to civility, decorum, and to the legal forms that depended upon their being preserved intact. It was, however, unimaginable to Julius Hoffman that the behavior of an unassimilated Jew was anything but subversive to American society. He preferred that defendants and witnesses suppress signs of their Jewishness (only a "clergyman" could wear a hat in court). For the judge no less than for the defendant, at that frenzied moment, to be a Jew and to respect American law seemed almost contradictory. Dual loyalty, after all, was still an issue. So the judge rejected symbols of Judaism as the defendant repudiated symbols of patriotism. Both Hoffmans, locked in their antagonistic embrace, seemed to agree that the assimilative force of law had temporarily reached its limits.

In calmer times, American Jews moved more easily between their communal and national identities. Judaism and American legalism co-existed in tranquility, with only the excessive piety of legalists like Frankfurter and Bickel to suggest some lingering internal turbulence. Yet their reverence seemed appropriate, for the power of American law was irresistible. Now that Jews no longer have reason to believe that justice is unavailable to them in court, the notion of "Jewish justice" has all but lost its meaning. Jewish arbitration tribunals have encouraged accommodation to American mores and function largely as adjuncts to Jewish social-service agencies. There are few Jewish communities where Jews are constrained from engaging in litigation with each other. Some, both secular and religious, do remain: in Hasidic Williamsburg

(Brooklyn), a man who rejects the Bet Din to sue another Jew is labeled a *moser* (informer) and treated with contemptuous silence by those who learn of his transgression. In the Diamond Dealers' Club, a variegated Jewish enclave in Manhattan that combines commercialism with Talmudic ethics, disputes never appear in court. The Club conciliates and arbitrates; its penalties are fines (payable to charity) or, in extreme cases, expulsion (with appropriate notice to diamond clubs throughout the world). The Bet Din, undercut by secularism and assimilation, has been confined to a tiny religious minority and its revival is not likely. But it still flickers with inspiration for some who yearn for Jewish harmony, morality, divinity, and community. Isaac Bashevis Singer, who remained captivated by memories of his father's rabbinical court, has predicted that "the court of the future will be based on the Bet Din, provided the world goes morally forward instead of backward. . . . The concept behind it is that there can be no justice without Godliness."[40]

All immigrant groups struggled with similar conflicts of autonomy and absorption. Their alternatives to the formal state legal system enabled them, at least for a time, to retain (or even develop) protective cohesion against threatening forces of acculturation. But as time eroded resistance to accommodation, alternative institutions were no longer necessary, or possible. Other affiliations—unions and professions—cut across ethnic lines, creating new loyalties and providing their own grievance procedures. The Americanization process, with its overriding emphasis on individual achievement, encouraged adversarial competitiveness and communal fragmentation.[41]

For a time, however, immigrants, like seventeenth-century colonists and nineteenth-century utopians, retained an alternative vision of social organization: not merely an aggregation of individuals but a community with shared values and commitments. Inevitably its members would quarrel among themselves, but when they did they turned toward each other, looking to restore group unity. Conflict was predictable; deviance lay in the pursuit of individual advantage against another group member beyond group boundaries. So Scandinavians replicated an earlier model of village serenity, secure from litigious warfare. The Chinese preserved the power of the patriarchal headman and the strength of associational life. (No other voluntary immigrant group used internal dispute settlement in such tenacious protection of a traditional structure of authority; in part, surely, because none was as blatantly mistreated in America as the Chinese.) Jews, consistent with their entire history in exile, reshaped traditional institutions to ease their transition as Americans. For all of them, and doubtless for others, litigiousness was intolerable as long as a community of common interest transcended individual self-interest. Once that community dissolved amid the promise of individual opportunity, the immigrants were Americans.

Chapter 4

The Commercialization of Community

Within a single generation, Roscoe Pound told a convention of lawyers in 1912, the American legal system had become the tarnished target of "unsparing criticism." Pound, professor of law at Harvard, was at the time one of the most outspoken critics. Just a few years earlier his own speech enumerating the causes of popular dissatisfaction with the administration of justice had so unsettled the American Bar Association that it refused to circulate his remarks to its membership. Pound described a horse-and-buggy legal system near collapse in an urban industrial society. Courts were congested; delay was endemic; costs were high; counsel was unavailable; entire areas of the substantive law were obsolete. Even sympathetic critics knew that "the wide disparity between the ability of the richer and poorer classes to utilize the machinery of the law" mocked the promise of equal justice and gravely menaced social stability.[1]

During the next decade there was a flurry of activity in legal circles to cope with a rigid, overburdened legal system: to devise new institutions, humane remedies, and flexible procedures that would make law and the administration of justice more responsive and efficient. It generated some of the most enduring legal reforms of the twentieth century: small-claims, domestic-relations, and juvenile courts; public defenders; legal aid societies; and industrial accident commissions. Administrative agencies and tribunals, at the state and national levels, eased the traditionally rigid, and increasingly dysfunctional, separation of legislative and judicial powers. Consequently, by World War I the modern regulatory state was sharply outlined, as Progressive reformers struggled to modernize an antiquated legal system and to create new institutions to resolve conflict, ameliorate grievances, and expand legal rights. Their remedies, however, produced more law (administrative regulation), more lawyers (legal aid), and more courts (especially for small claims)—not less.[2] Reorganized courts, new tribunals, additional judges, and streamlined procedures might mitigate costly delays and interminable appeals. Legal aid societies might provide poor people with attorneys for their day in court. Administrative discretion could soften rigid governmental processes. But was expanded legal regulation and control, however accessible, efficient, and flexible, a remedy—or another problem?

It did not take long for Pound to discover limits to legal action. By 1916, he warned against inflated expectations of social change through law. "When men demand much of law, when they seek to devolve upon it the whole burden of social control, . . . enforcement of law comes to involve many difficulties." As regulatory activity increased and legal controls expanded, complaints of non-enforcement multiplied, friction between regulator and regulated increased, and the volume of disputes soared. Other institutions (Pound identified religion and the family) atrophied. The more law, the more dissatisfaction with it. There were, Pound concluded, "intrinsic limitations upon effective legal action"; not every social problem had a legal solution. The recurrent dialectic between—in Pound's words—"justice without law" and "justice according to law" had surfaced once again.[3]

As dissatisfaction with legal institutions increased during the early decades of the twentieth century, there was renewed interest in alternatives to litigation, especially conciliation and arbitration. Both were touted as speedy, inexpensive procedures to dispense with lawyers and reduce the acrimonious, costly delays that suffused litigation. But they originated in separate constituencies to serve divergent interests. Conciliation was a reform offered by the legal community to a marginal clientele; it was designed to resolve the claims of poor people who could not afford counsel, and who were especially victimized by court congestion and delay. Arbitration, by contrast, expressed the preference of commercial interests, especially in New York, for self-regulation untrammeled by the intrusion of law and lawyers. Consistent with these differences of origin and purpose, conciliation limped along in a state of neglect, while arbitration flourished to become a national institution—deeply enmeshed, ironically, in the legal system. Their respective histories illuminate the first modern attempts to divert disputes from a legal system that was perceived as too expensive, contentious, and inefficient to resolve them satisfactorily.

Conciliation was part of a package of reforms designed to alleviate procedural injustices that bore down most heavily upon the urban poor. Along with legal aid, small-claims courts, and public defenders, it was intended to undercut the claim that justice was available only in proportion to the ability to pay for it.[4] The modern conciliation movement began in 1913 in Cleveland, where a conciliation branch of the municipal court was authorized to assist litigants who were unable to obtain lawyers to settle their small claims. All claims for thirty-five dollars or less were entered on the conciliation docket; parties were encouraged to appear before a municipal judge without lawyers; in the absence of formal legal procedure, the judge, relying upon an "appeal to common sense" to resolve the disagreement, tried to arouse amicable feelings and suppress fighting instincts. Conciliation procedure was voluntary and formless, intended to encourage disputants to compromise their differences. Judgments rested entirely upon the consent of the parties; if conciliation failed, the dispute went to trial.[5]

The conciliation idea spread slowly during the next decade. The Cleveland plan provided a model for Chicago, where a similar program was implemented two years later. In New York, the state bar association endorsed conciliation as an alternative to what one member described as "the hell of litigation." In Philadelphia, the Municipal Court established a special division for conciliation, small claims, and legal aid. And in Iowa, controversies involving less than one hundred dollars were consigned to conciliation at the discretion of the judge. The presence of lawyers was discouraged; the object was "to get the parties themselves to meet and talk over their differences."[6]

The rhetoric of conciliation emphasized harmony and amity as alternatives to conflict, which litigation encouraged even as it provided legal forms and procedures for containing disputes. "Disputes run all too easily into class, religious, and racial animosities and prejudices," warned law reformer Reginald Heber Smith. Litigation tended only "to inflame and perpetuate quarrels"; conciliation, however, offered "moderation, forebearance, mutual adjustment and honorable compromise," thereby avoiding the bitterness of a contested trial. It was, according to an editorial written in praise of the Cleveland experiment, "a movement toward justice in spite of lawyers."[7]

Proponents of conciliation mixed a genuine commitment to inexpensive, informal dispute settlement with a strong aversion to the "ignorant" and "laboring" classes who would benefit from it (but were not consulted about its use). It was only a short step from this defense of conciliation to its justification as an antidote to radical criticism of American legal institutions, a consuming concern of bench and bar after World War I. "We were constantly harassed by men on street corners talking of the imperfections of the judicial system," complained a Minnesota judge, who described conciliation in his state as "a great success." An Idaho attorney concurred: ". . . we have a great many I.W.W.'s and others . . . who raise an outcry against the courts." But informal procedure, which cut through "technical rules" to reach "substantial justice," might undercut that criticism.[8]

Because alternatives to litigation revived within a highly developed legal culture, conciliation—and arbitration—had to be reconciled with legal norms and values, and rendered acceptable to the legal profession. In the colonial era, just the reverse had been true: legal dispute resolution gained acceptance slowly amid considerable resistance in tightly structured homogeneous communities. By the twentieth century, however, with the balance tipped decisively toward legalized dispute settlement, it was the legal culture that set the terms of debate. Conciliation deviated from the trial-by-battle model: there were no formal procedures, jurors, or lawyers. How, then, to render it acceptable—or harmless?

Smith, in a series of articles advocating conciliation, insisted that it merely complemented the judicial system; if it failed, "the work of the court remains, the function of the courts is not altered, nor is their service impaired." He tried to mollify his legal audience, worried lest the power of judges and lawyers be reduced, by defining conciliation as a preliminary judicial procedure for settling litigation, not a separate proceeding conducted in independent tribunals.[9] Herbert Harley, another vigorous proponent, concurred with Smith on the advantages of judicial control over conciliation and small-claims proceedings, especially at a time when judges were threatened by the loss of jurisdiction "rightfully theirs." Harley recalled how an aroused public had torn personal injury litigation from courts and given it to workmen's compensation commissions. History would repeat itself, he predicted, unless judges asserted their power as conciliators in small-claims proceedings.[10]

The legal profession was assured that with judges in control, justice—even in informal proceedings—would not be administered "as the arbitrary ruling of an untrammeled despot," but "according to the principles of substantive law." Nor would lawyers be adversely affected by conciliation proceedings. Conciliation "would take no money out of the pockets of the Bar," a New York lawyer reassured his colleagues. Indeed, the elimination of lawyers from the unsavory breeding ground of the municipal "pettifogger's court" was a blessing that would enhance professional prestige. As one lawyers' committee on conciliation concluded: "the better members of our profession have no ardent desire to try $25 cases in a small claims court and . . . it is the less desirable fraction of the bar that the small claims court want to keep out." As an extra dividend, small-claims litigation would be removed from juries, which cause "all the flub-dub of the court-room, giving trials their histrionic and time-consuming character."[11]

The appeal of conciliation (to lawyers) was evident. But there was a fatal flaw in its theory and practice: it was alien to its presumed beneficiaries. Except in Minnesota and North Dakota, where conciliation tapped cultural values of the local Scandinavian communities, it was provided for disputants within a framework of legal proceedings; it was not their own indigenous alternative. Conciliation expressed the values of the professionals who espoused it, not those of the urban lower class for whom it was designed. Consequently, conciliation lapsed as a weak adjunct to the small-claims court reform movement, confined largely to claims and disputes that were deemed too trivial for most lawyers and judges to bother with.

Advocates of small-claims courts and conciliation procedure rested their proposals upon assumptions about the legal system that limited the scope and weakened the impact of their reforms. Fully committed to the legal system, they believed it to be fundamentally sound: the substantive law, said Reginald Heber Smith, was a "remarkably satisfactory human achievement." They thought the only issues were technical and procedural: how to administer law efficiently, without congestion and delay. Once these were identified as the crucial problems, solutions that required changes in the substantive law could be disregarded. Rather, the "judicial *machine*" required overhauling and retuning. Small-claims courts and conciliation would satisfy the need for procedural and administrative reform in the processing of "minor" disputes without risking unnecessary (and dangerous) substantive alterations.[12]

Once the small claims of poor people were designated as "simple" or "petty," it was easy to consign them to informal resolution and sidestep such procedural guarantees as the right to counsel or trial by jury. The result was a two-tier justice system, with conciliation as an alternative for those who could not afford to buy the protection offered by the legal system. Whether the disputes of poor people were channeled into the formal legal labyrinth or diverted to the speedier, informal procedures of conciliation, poor disputants were disadvantaged.[13]

While conciliation was quickly relegated to the periphery of a legalistic culture, commercial arbitration enjoyed striking success within that culture. Its revival was nourished by the convergence of business organization and government regulation during the early years of the twentieth century. After a turbulent era of competitive disorder following the Civil War, business consolidation made self-regulation possible. By the 1920s there was a high level of industrial self-government. Indeed, business interests were equated with the national interest; the ideal society was seen as a benevolent business commonwealth (although, to be sure, uncommon wealth was reserved for businessmen). As business power expanded, however, government regulatory power (with considerable lag) also expanded in an effort to contain it. But the stronger the regulatory state, the stronger the desire for spheres of voluntary activity beyond its control. The growth of the regulatory state unsettled advocates of commercial autonomy, who turned to arbitration as a shield against government intrusion. Arbitration fit neatly into their vision of industrial planning; it permitted businessmen to solve their own problems "in their own way—without resort to the clumsy and heavy hand of Government."[14] Commercial arbitration revived as the indigenous demand of powerful economic groups who formed their own consensual communities of profit. Appropriately, in a modern business society, the strongest shared sense of community originated in the New York Chamber of Commerce.

The Chamber's arbitration committees, dating from 1768, had evolved into a permanent tribunal toward the end of the nineteenth century. Although parties might withdraw at any time prior to an award, and the awards were not enforceable, there was a high degree of compliance with Chamber decisions. "The merchant may fearlessly come into this court without a lawyer,"

members were told; "if the right be on his side," he would even
prevail against adversarial ingenuity. The Chamber's arbitration
judge warned against "the skill and technicality that prevail in
forensic contests," which produced results "hostile to the true
principles of justice." His tribunal relied upon "common sense"
to reach the merits of the dispute, providing "no opportunity for
craftiness or trick to obscure or entangle them with cobwebs."
Judicial procedures only "darkened the temples of justice with
the mould of the past"; they were unsuited to "the progress and
exigencies of commerce." Despite this glowing description of the
wonders of arbitration, the Chamber tribunal was seldom used
by the beginning of the twentieth century. Arbitration was
neglected in a dynamic, chaotic era of expanding industrial capitalism, when businessmen were too engaged in their own market
struggles to perceive many interests in common with their competitors.[15]

Before World War I, commercial arbitration was confined to
trade associations whose members engaged in the continuous sale
or trade of a special product, commodity, or security. (Arbitration in the New York Stock Exchange, the Chicago Board of
Trade, and the fur and silk industries dated back to the nineteenth
century.) In such tightly organized associations the value of an
enduring commercial relationship far exceeded the value of a
particular commodity. Without the internal resolution of disputes
through arbitration, litigation would inevitably promote "hard
feeling and ultimate disruption" of the bonds that sustained commercial relationships. As long as disputes were settled within the
association, members were assured that their shared customs,
however idiosyncratic, would be respected. Trade custom, which
facilitated amicable relations between buyer and seller, offered
far more security than the mysterious, and threatening, procedures of the law.[16]

Chamber arbitration was revived at the instigation of Charles
L. Bernheimer, president of a cotton-goods concern, who was
frustrated by the costs, delays, and uncertainties of commercial
litigation. Bernheimer touted the virtues of arbitration, which

resolved disputes "in a rough and ready 'Squire Justice' fashion wherein ordinary common sense, knowledge of human nature, a clean cut sense of commercial equity, patience and forebearance produce the results desired" by businessmen. More powerful than "the force of law," reported his Chamber of Commerce arbitration committee, was "the collective conscience of a group."[17] Other businessmen were also discovering the advantages of commercial arbitration. In Illinois, where arbitration by the Chicago Board of Trade helped to rationalize the commodities market, various commodities exchanges used its arbitration processes to maintain common standards and tight discipline among members. "Why waste time, energy and money in court trials?" read a letter of inquiry to "Mr. Business Man" in Illinois. Arbitration "does not result in enmity between the parties, as does the ordinary law suit." Instead, it offered expertise, business efficiency, and just results.[18]

Preliminary support for the principle of arbitration came from an unexpected source: the legal profession. As the administration of justice deteriorated in urban America, lawyers were thrown on the defensive. They conceded (at least in the privacy of their own company), that there was " a widespread feeling throughout the country that our bench and bar are not meeting the demands of the present age, that there has been manifest a growing distrust of our courts and a growing disrespect for our laws."[19] At the annual meeting of the Missouri Bar Association in 1914 Percy Werner, a St. Louis attorney, proposed a "simple, dignified, honest, conciliatory, and democratic" procedure for the resolution of private disputes. Ordinary citizens were entitled to a procedure "free from technicality and mystery," which cut "to the marrow of a controversy in a simple, speedy, direct manner." As government regulation increased, Werner observed, courts were inundated with an unprecedented volume of public-law issues, ranging from labor-management conflict to public utilities regulation to social legislation for working women and children. To reduce judicial congestion the ordinary private disputes of individuals should be diverted to voluntary tribunals for arbitration by a lawyer, chosen by the disputants' attorneys. Not only would these tribunals serve the public; they would benefit bench and bar. Public respect for the judiciary would increase as overcrowded dockets diminished. Since only attorneys with "character and learning" would serve as arbitrators, "suspicion and reproach" of the bar would recede.[20]

The New York Chamber of Commerce expressed interest in Werner's proposal, noting the opportunity for "cooperative usefulness between commercial organizations and the legal profession." The New York State Bar Association established a new committee to consider a range of alternatives that its members proposed for preventing unnecessary litigation: conciliation courts; Mormon-style mediation; arbitration; and specialized merchants' tribunals.[21] Arbitration captured the committee's interest, but lawyers and businessmen wanted different results from it. Lawyers, defensive about criticism, were eager to improve their public image, without losing clients, while retaining control over dispute resolution. Businessmen, apprehensive about outside intrusion, wanted expeditious, inexpensive justice which comported with commercial practice, free of external legal constraints.

The critical development in their merger of interests occurred in 1920, when New York enacted a statute providing that agreements to arbitrate future disputes were irrevocable and enforceable. This statute climaxed a persistent effort by the Chamber and the bar association for legislative relief from common-law doctrine, dating from Lord Coke's opinion in *Vynior's Case* (1609), which encouraged easy revocability of arbitration agreements by refusing to enforce them. Julius Henry Cohen (counsel to the Chamber, a bar association member, and an earlier advocate of *Kehillah* arbitration) had published an exhaustive study of the legal history of arbitration, in effect a lawyer's brief to overturn *Vynior's Case*, still the controlling decision in American arbitration law. American procedure still permitted either party, at any time between submission of the dispute to arbitration and the final award, to revoke the agreement to arbitrate. Cohen concluded that revocability was "a legal anachronism"; his book bolstered the campaign for statutory arbitration and his draft bill prodded the legislature to enact the 1920 statute.[22] With the new law, agreements to arbitrate future disputes were, for the first time, legally binding and judicially enforceable.

Commercial arbitration, Cohen insisted, provided a necessary alternative to the deficiencies of legal procedure and to the intrusiveness of government regulation. He relied upon private agreements between parties, supported by contract law, as the key to economic harmony. (Proponents of the legislation did not dwell on the prospect that an agreement to arbitrate, exacted from a weaker party, might constitute economic duress without legal redress.) A binding agreement to arbitrate future disputes, legally enforceable like any other contract, promised to insulate private rule-making from government control and to remove business disputes from the courts. Yet at the same time that the new law "gives to people who want to keep out of the courts an opportunity for settling their differences . . . it puts the [arbitration] process under a measurable supervision of the courts and adds the power of the judicial process to the words of the parties themselves."[23] Binding arbitration agreements absorbed the best of two worlds: they combined the benign fiction of voluntary consent with the stringent reality of legal enforcement. They thereby contained the appropriate blend of business autonomy and judicial control.

Although the New York law provided the legal framework for the development of modern arbitration, the uneasiness of some lawyers, fearful of displacement from the dispute-settlement process, jeopardized its success. During a vigorous debate in the American Bar Association one elderly attorney warned that arbitration required a man to sign away his "birth right"—his right to a court trial. An overwrought lawyer from Massachusetts saw a menacing parallel between contractual arbitration and the destruction of legal procedure in the Soviet Union, "where they have taken the lawyers and put them out to work in the fields and factories, where they have closed down the courts." Why have laws, law schools, and bar associations at all, he wondered, "if by one fell blow you are to say that lawyers are of no account?"[24] Fear of lost legal business, and lost professional respect, echoed through the arbitration debates.

Charles L. Bernheimer, the leading spokesman for arbitration within the Chamber of Commerce, tried to soothe professional apprehensions. "We regard the lawyer as our friend, as our faithful co-worker, co-builder and adviser in trade and industry," he told a conference of bar association delegates. He reminded the lawyers of their low public image but promised that a united front with businessmen, working to prevent unnecessary litigation, would restore respect for the law and confidence in the legal profession. Arbitration and law practice were merely "different phases of the same endeavor." Arbitration hearings were as dignified as judicial proceedings; arbitrators, like judges, would "avoid compromise and splitting of differences." (This reassurance was intended to appease legal traditionalists who still believed in unambiguous black-letter law, declared by judges who discovered it without any exercise of discretion.) Businessmen, he concluded, should create a demand for arbitration "as we create a demand for a new brand of merchandise"; lawyers, with nothing to fear from it, should support it.[25]

Some leaders of the New York and national bar—among them Charles Evans Hughes, John W. Davis, and Charles C. Burlingham—cooperated to establish the Arbitration Society of America. Its active leader, Moses H. Grossman, was a former municipal court judge who was disturbed by public disrespect for law, apprehensive about social upheaval if appropriate remedies were not implemented, committed to business self-regulation, and eager for cooperation between lawyers and businessmen. At a series of meetings to secure professional support for arbitration, Grossman reminded lawyers that court congestion had worsened steadily, resulting in overworked judges and three-year delays. Everyone knew that "there is something wrong somewhere." One lawyer had even warned Grossman that "if we don't abolish the abuses, the public will gradually abolish us."[26]

If delay was dangerous, the prospective absence of lawyers

from dispute settlement was, to Grossman, "simply ridiculous." They already were excluded from arbitration proceedings in trade associations, which resolved thousands of disagreements annually. Lawyers "of character, of ability, of judicial temperament and discernment" should have the opportunity to participate in commercial arbitration. Grossman's argument was palpably elitist—and legalistic. He condemned the "ignorance, if not sheer stupidity," of juries; arbitrators, by contrast, would be drawn from the respectable ranks of middle-class professionals. Indeed, every able lawyer was a potential arbitrator; once the Hugheses, Cravaths, and Guthries—Grossman chose carefully from the professional elite—came to the rescue of beleaguered courts, disrespect for law, which encouraged "bolshevistic propaganda" and provided "the cornerstone of revolution," would diminish.[27]

The Arbitration Society sponsored a Public Tribunal of Justice, "a People's Tribunal" for prompt, inexpensive settlement of all civil (but non-matrimonial) controversies. It was promoted as a "common sense proceeding" in which "the facts alone will prevail . . . unshackled by legal rules and considered by arbitrators who aim at simple justice without regard to legal technicalities." More than one favorable editorial welcomed the opportunity it afforded to eliminate "trickster and shyster" lawyers, who "lie in wait" to prey on poor people's claims. The tribunal, aptly described as "a court without lawyers, formed by lawyers," started slowly. After more than a year of operation in New York its settlement rate approximated the pace of a state supreme court judge (450 cases annually)—hardly a dramatic improvement, but not fatal to the hopes of its advocates.[28]

Challenges to the tribunal quickly arose on its commercial and legal flanks: from businessmen who preferred to exclude lawyers, and from lawyers who resented the diversion of disputes into non-legal channels. At one meeting, an officer of the Silk Association, which had adopted arbitration in 1898 to "make people settle their disputes themselves," told Grossman that "common ordinary businessmen can settle these matters better than you [lawyers] can." Disputes were resolved according to trade customs and "the ordinary understanding of what is right and wrong." But the moment a lawyer participated, "he is going to dominate the situation and bind the thing up with technicalities and precedents," rather than yield to business expertise. Lawyers, predictably, were unpersuaded: the judgment of "plain men" who claimed to possess "a precious jewel which they call common-sense," one retorted, was no substitute for "the magnificent structure of the law . . . which has built up civilization."[29]

Commercial interests preferred to confine arbitration to their own trade associations and to chambers of commerce. In these forums, where lawyers were less welcome, businessmen retained the power to resolve disputes according to trade practice rather than legal principle. Proponents of non-legal commercial arbitration challenged the Society in 1925 with their own organization, the Arbitration Foundation. Led by Bernheimer, who chaired the Chamber of Commerce arbitration committee, it represented an attempt to retain business control over the arbitration of commercial disputes. As businessmen and lawyers struggled for control over commercial arbitration the arbitration movement, dedicated to dispute settlement, suddenly found itself dispute-ridden. Appropriately, however, the disputing parties agreed to resolve their differences through arbitration. The Foundation appointed three businessmen; the Society chose an architect, a banker, and a law-school dean. (These six selected Lucius R. Eastman, a businessman *and* lawyer, as their chairman.) After nearly a year of negotiation, they reached a merger agreement: in 1926 the American Arbitration Association was formed. Consolidation was an indisputable victory for bench and bar. Lawyers and judges were conspicuously present in the new Association. Not only were they board members, policy-makers, and arbitrators; they even served as counsel in arbitration proceedings. The institutional framework for the legalization of commercial dispute settlement was securely in place.[30]

In the 1920s the remnants of the communitarian impulse were preserved in the idea of a cohesive commercial community. Business literature resounded with the themes of unity and harmony—to be sure, in pursuit of maximum private profit and minimum government regulation. Secretary of Commerce Herbert Hoover captured this blend when he commended the rapid growth of arbitration as an example of business cooperation with an "ethical function" no less than economic objectives. The Chamber of Commerce articulated the ethical content of arbitration when it referred to "good will between men" and "the sense of Commercial Honor in the business community," which encouraged businessmen to submit to "the morally binding effect" of arbitration agreements rather than seek refuge in legal technicalities. Platitudes perhaps, but also expressive of a genuine commitment to a harmonious commercial community. "Next to war," declared the Bureau of Foreign and Domestic Commerce, "commercial litigation is the largest single item of preventable waste in civilization."[31] Businessmen had become the newest American communitarians.

Although many businessmen may have preferred commercial arbitration free of legal constraints, they could not maintain total independence from the legal system. The business community was too internally fragmented to contain every dispute within arbitration proceedings; the pursuit of redress in court still was an available option. Lawyers, tenaciously retaining their role in dispute settlement, remained suspicious of commercial arbitration until they were assured an important place in its processes. The price for their cooperation was high: commercial arbitration was quickly and thoroughly legalized. By 1930, in fact, it was nothing less than "expert adjudication with all the safeguards of law."[32] The active participation of lawyers, and a voluminous case law of arbitration, measured the dramatic legalization of the arbitration process during the 1920s. Businessmen learned that their new statutory charter of freedom might ensnare them in a legal web.

What law protected, after all, law also controlled. An arbitration agreement, Julius Henry Cohen insisted, was a business contract which should be "as inviolable as any other business contract." Its inviolability, however, depended upon judicial sanctions. Cohen was pleased that arbitration proceedings "from beginning to end may be brought under the supervision of the courts if either party deems it necessary."[33] The new arbitration legislation, which assured judicial supervision and enforcement, transformed arbitration from a voluntary alternative to "the quasi-judicial branch of industrial society." But as arbitration became more deeply enmeshed in the legal system, to the point where it even served as the preliminary stage of a trial, the advantages of an informal alternative form of dispute settlement receded. The New York statute triggered an enormous volume of litigation, testing the enforcement, scope, method, and review of arbitration. The presence of an available legal forum encouraged participants in arbitration to litigate to determine how to fill arbitrator vacancies, whether stenographic notes of arbitration proceedings should be taken, and, predictably, whether counsel should be present. An occasional horror made arbitration resemble Dickens's *Jarndyce v. Jarndyce*: one case, which moved through courts in two states and came twice before a circuit court of appeals, generated five opinions (three of which concerned technical jurisdictional questions) and was still unresolved after five years. (A century earlier a Connecticut judge had warned, presciently, that with unlimited appeals, arbitration, "instead of being an expeditious mode of settling controversies, would only be calculated to lengthen and perplex them.")[34]

The establishment of the American Arbitration Association symbolized and accelerated the shift to legalized arbitration. Chamber of Commerce arbitration had been informal, flexible, and largely unencumbered by lawyers or precedent. Similarly, trade association arbitration was oriented toward business custom; sanctions were disciplinary, not legal. But the American Arbitration Association, lacking any particular set of trade norms to guide it, was law-oriented from the outset (and may have attracted a clientele that preferred speedy, inexpensive dispute settlement but was unwilling to abandon the benefits of legal counsel and the possibility of judicial review when it was disadvantaged in arbitration). Attentive to the prospect of judicial review, the association moved carefully within the boundaries of legal rules, precedent, and procedural due process.[35]

The commitment to legal norms encouraged the presence of lawyers, who, of course, reinforced legal norms. Lawyers participated as counsel in Association arbitration at a steadily ascending rate (from 36 percent in 1927 to 91 percent twenty years later). The greater the financial amount in dispute, the more likely lawyers were to appear as arbitrators. Consequently, commercial arbitration, historically an alternative to legal control, quickly and increasingly resembled formal legal dispute settlement.[36]

Legal arbitration reached formal maturity by 1930. Wesley Sturges's thousand-page *Treatise on Commercial Arbitration and Awards* was its symbolic testimonial. Sturges was a law professor at Yale; his volume was methodologically and substantively indistinguishable from any other legal treatise, even if his subject, until just a decade earlier, was an alternative mode of voluntary dispute settlement. Although it was not his intention, Sturges provided abundant evidence to document the tenacious resistance of courts to their competitors, the determined efforts of bench and bar to control through the legal process what they could not eradicate, and the persistent willingness of business disputants to litigate. The thousands of case citations amassed by Sturges prompted Nathan Isaacs, professor of business law at the Harvard Business School, to observe in a review: "There is irony in the fate of one who takes precautions to avoid litigation by submitting to arbitration, and who, as a reward for his pains, finds himself eventually in court fighting not on the merits of his case but on the merits of the arbitration." The result, Isaacs suggested, was "a monumental tragicomedy" that demonstrated the success of law in "thwarting legitimate efforts to escape its tortuous procedure."[37]

The bubble of arbitration euphoria was punctured by the Depression. As the stock market plummeted, so did respect for the infallible wisdom of business leadership. The business of

America was business, Calvin Coolidge had insisted, and factories might be described as temples where workers worshipped (for twelve or fourteen hours daily), but after 1929 such aphorisms sounded increasingly hollow. Critics chipped away at arbitration and then, in the full flush of New Deal liberalism, launched a frontal assault against it as a bastion of business power insulated from social responsibility and contrary to the public interest.

The critique emerged moderately in 1930. Isaacs's review of the Sturges treatise pointed to the irony of excessive legalization. Philip G. Phillips, who analyzed the paradox of legal enforcement of voluntary proceedings, suggested that "enforced arbitration"—imposed by one contracting party upon another, backed by judicial sanctions—"is not arbitration."[38] The first year of the New Deal marked the divide; thereafter, criticism of arbitration was sharper and cut deeper. Indeed, the terms of the debate were decisively altered. The problem, freshly perceived by New Dealers for whom corporate business was the enemy, was not the legalization of arbitration but the immunity it provided business from public regulation. To them, arbitration symbolized the deficiencies of a laissez-faire economy; law, constantly criticized by liberals since the turn of the century for retarding progress, was now rediscovered as an instrument of reform that protected the public interest against private rule-making.

In a series of law review articles during 1933–34, Phillips offered an analysis of arbitration from the perspective of liberal legalism. Like Isaacs, he became less enamored of arbitration once regulation of corporate power became the major political issue of the Depression. Before he joined the New Deal as counsel to the National Labor Relations Board, he had supported legal encouragement of arbitration; thereafter he was its most outspoken critic.[39] Combining broad rhetorical strokes with tightly reasoned policy analysis, Phillips attacked "business propagandists" who had transformed an available legal tool for settling disputes into "a fetish" and a "magic nostrum" for curing legal ills. Statutory arbitration, he suggested, was the product of "a somewhat bewildered legislature [acting] at the high-powered lobbying behest

of sincere, but nonetheless erroneous, business philosophers."
Arbitration meant decision by "inspiration," rather than "utili-
tarian justice by law and social policy." A public system of
courts was a fundamental social necessity in a democratic society:
"there alone the public . . . can find protection."[40] Phillips defended the "socialized orderly process of the law" against "the
laissez-faire individualism of lay arbitration." Law—standardized,
public, and organic—expressed social policy; arbitration, which
shielded trade practices from public scrutiny and permitted
powerful interests to insulate their disciplinary procedures, substituted private will for social control. Protection of the public
interest required more judicial supervision of private activity,
not less, because "our law in most cases is good and fits modern
conditions."[41] It was not law against justice, as defenders of arbitration had insisted, but legal rules—and the rule of law—against
laissez-faire individualism and corporate autonomy.

The menace of fascism strengthened the critical reassessment
of arbitration. The growth of German business cartels, and their
complicity with the Nazi regime, cast a shadow across unregulated corporate activities. Suddenly, arbitration loomed as an
extra-legal instrument of private business power. As its reach
extended beyond the interested parties of a particular dispute to
encompass entire industries, the danger of unchecked corporate
power increased. Dominant business interests, it was argued,
would use compulsory arbitration clauses as a shield for their
efforts to control prices, suppress competition, and thwart legislative regulation while they removed their private rules from
public supervision. Lawless private government would inevitably
follow.[42]

But commercial arbitration already was too deeply entrenched
to be dislodged. After a period of competitive jostling, the legal
system and the business system worked out a *modus vivendi*,
which permitted substantial private autonomy within a legal
framework. Commercial arbitration survived the New Deal at-
tack; by the 1950s, according to one estimate, nearly three-
quarters of all commercial litigation was being diverted from

courts to arbitrators. Some lawyers remained uneasy with what they still perceived as a persistent "flight not only from our law courts . . . but also from our law men." Arbitration, belatedly recognized as a shield to protect the exercise of private power, prompted the troubled inquiry: "To what extent shall the modern business institution be autonomous from the state?"[43] Like so many other questions about arbitration, the answer has varied according to time and context. Law could not entirely stifle alternatives, a fear of apprehensive businessmen belied by the flourishing practice of commercial arbitration. Nor could arbitration altogether elude law, as worried lawyers anticipated. A disadvantaged or disappointed business disputant could always carry an appeal to court—and many continued to do so. The marriage of commercial and legal convenience has endured.

During the twentieth century, the possibilities for escape from legalized dispute settlement, so ample throughout earlier American history, have steadily narrowed. Commercial arbitration began as an effort to tame the "growing monster" of litigation by "the gentle practice of arbitration."[44] But the rule of law, and the role of lawyers and judges in its preservation, easily survived its newest challenge. In fact, the monster nibbled at arbitration until the similarities were more conspicuous than the differences.

Conciliation and commercial arbitration provide suggestive comparative models for the possibilities and limits of non-legal dispute settlement in modern America. The conciliation experiment worked where it was indigenous to an immigrant community, but the attempt of legal professionals to impose it upon poor people was unsuccessful. By contrast, commercial arbitration expressed the needs of highly organized segments of the business community. Yet it could not have flourished without legal support, which simultaneously constricted its potential as an alternative dispute-settlement system. These early-twentieth-century experiments suggest that if the impulse toward justice without law is periodically irresistible, the legalization of dispute settlement seems inexorable in our modern culture.

Chapter 5

The Legalization
of Community

In 1958, at the urging of the American Bar Association, President
Eisenhower designated May Day as Law Day, an annual occasion
for celebratory reminders of American dedication to the rule of
law. At the time, the historical sources of alternative dispute
settlement seemed depleted, if not exhausted. Utopian experiments
were moribund; the children and grandchildren of immigrants
had become Americans; principles of secular pluralism prevailed
in American society. By now, the predominance of law as a
cultural force is beyond dispute. It might be measured by the
assertive role of the Supreme Court (whether heroic or villainous
is beyond the point); by the hypnotic allure of the courtroom
trial as a staple of national melodrama; by the national obsession
with rights and rules; by the astonishing attractiveness of the
legal profession as a career choice. No longer is it possible to reflect seriously about American culture without accounting for the
centrality of law in American history and society, and in the
mythology of American uniqueness and grandeur.

Ever since the turn of the century, however, law reformers
have worried incessantly about the capacity of the American
legal system to deliver on its promises. Expectations of equal
justice were nurtured but they could not be fulfilled in a society
where economic and political resources were unequally distributed. Constricted by political and legal blinders, the Progressive

reform vision still sets narrow limits to the possibilities for change. The more inadequacies legal institutions demonstrate, the more legal remedies are provided to cure them. Administrative agencies, legal aid societies, and small-claims courts endure; but so do the problems they were designed to alleviate. Tinkering with the legal machinery by adding more lawyers and courts has not removed the disparities of wealth and power that produce its malfunctions. Periodic redefinitions of lawyers' ethical responsibilities are a reflexive response to public criticism, not a remedy for the defects of the adversary process. The problems of injustice were passed along, a Progressive legacy of failure, to a subsequent generation of law reformers, who again have turned to alternative processes to rescue the legal system from the enduring defects of constricted access, high cost, excessive delay, and congestive overload.

For nearly twenty years the idea of alternative dispute settlement has shimmered elusively like a desert mirage. The first call for its revival arose from the euphoric hope that burst forth during the sixties, when community empowerment became a salient theme of political reform. New ideas about popular justice floated on the exhilarating prospect of political change to restore neighborhood energy and purpose, even in the deepest recesses of urban blight. A sweeping agenda of law reform included proposals for neighborhood law firms (the germinal idea for the federal legal services program) and a neighborhood court system. Neighborhood "reconciliation boards" (the term used by Sargent Shriver, whose Office of Economic Opportunity supported the development of community dispute-settlement programs) would encourage city residents to channel conflict into "locally based and locally responsive tribunals" designed to promote "the democratization of justice." In a series of seminal articles advocating these proposals, lawyers Edgar and Jean Cahn drew important distinctions (often ignored by subsequent enthusiasts) between indigenous neighborhood disputes that were appropriate for community processes, and grievances directed against external sources of control, which required access to litigation. Within a neighborhood, local mores might be more effective than legal rules; but once disputes cut across community boundaries, redress of grievances required legal sanctions. Even as the Cahns looked beyond the strictures of the formal legal system, however, they were troubled by the idea of lay participation in dispute settlement. Caught between their professional values and community commitments, they located their community court proposal solidly within a framework of legalistic assumptions, procedural safeguards, and judicial appeals.[1] So, at the very moment of inception, alternative dispute settlement was pulled back into the courts—a tendency that became even more pronounced as the search for alternatives accelerated.

Independent of the Cahns' proposal, the American Friends Service Committee developed a plan for citizen dispute settlement that drew upon a mixture of African tribal practice and a mediation program within the black community of Chester, Pennsylvania. Its underlying principle was a conception of disputes as a form of property that "should belong to the community rather than the formalized judicial system." These proponents of community empowerment criticized courts as remote, inaccessible institutions that represented the interests of the state and the values of legal professionals. Once conflict entered the courthouse, the nature of a dispute was transformed as disputants were required to defer to professionals who translated the social complexities of their disagreements into legal issues. Legal training, one critic suggested, created "a trained incapacity in letting the parties decide what *they* think is relevant." If communities could contain the conflict of their members, and encourage citizen participation in its resolution, they might preserve a vital source of their own empowerment.[2]

Communitarian euphoria for alternative dispute settlement was short-lived. After 1968, when simmering rage exploded in urban ghettos blighted by poverty and racism, the justification for alternatives quickly shifted. Informal mediation was now promoted as "an alternative to violence," designed especially to coax civil rights activists and their angry ghetto constituencies from the streets to quieter sanctuaries. If "minor disputes" were contained, "far more dangerous conflicts" would dissolve. New proposals were shaped by the alluring historical analogy of labor-management relations, which seemed to suggest that workers and employers, who once were locked into violent instability, had finally been rescued by the institutionalization of mediation and arbitration during the New Deal. But the analogy, like others that inspired alternative dispute-settlement efforts, was flawed. In the thirties, sweeping changes in the *law* of labor relations, providing new legal rights backed by strong government sanctions, required employers to bargain collectively. The collective bargaining process, supported by a legal framework, contained their hostility to negotiation. Community conflict in the sixties, by contrast, erupted without any prior or continuing relationship between disputants (perhaps the unique feature of collective bargaining). Nothing in urban ghettos remotely resembled the exclusive jurisdiction of bargaining units that assured stability within a labor-management context defined by legal obligations.[3]

Communitarian impulses proved to be too weak to sustain the revival of alternative dispute settlement, while urban violence was too explosive to be contained by so benign a process as mediation. (By far the largest role in urban conflict resolution, from Watts to Harlem, was played by the police, the National Guard, and the army.) Amid spiraling cycles of violence that threatened to overwhelm established legal institutions of conflict resolution, the pursuit of alternatives persisted. After the urban riots, dispute-settlement analogies were reshuffled. Richard Danzig, a young lawyer with the New York Rand Corporation, presented the idea of an African tribal moot as part of a proposal for the decentralized administration of urban criminal justice. Among the Kpelle of Liberia the moot was an alternative to the Liberian court system, a Western legal imposition. It provided a process of therapeutic resolution of interpersonal and family disputes. Grievances were aired in the complainant's home, with disputants interspersed among kinsmen and spectators in a ritualized process of tribal conciliation. There were no judgments of guilt; only rewards for compliance with tribal norms that stressed the value of social harmony. "Despite the differences between a tribal culture and our own," Danzig asked, "isn't there a place for a community moot in our judicial system?" An urban moot, attentive to the values of the neighborhood, might substitute "consensual solutions" for the conflict that already had wracked American cities.[4]

Although the Kpelle process sounded sufficiently alluring for the Danzig proposal to be cited in virtually every subsequent plan for community dispute settlement, it was precisely the differences between Kpelle culture and American cities that made it impossible to replicate here. The Kpelle moot thrived as an indigenous expression of tribal coherence, and as a genuine alternative to the official Liberian courts. Danzig's community moot, however, was designed to make the local judiciary more effective. It would remain solidly entrenched within the criminal justice system, with referrals from police, courts, and social agencies. For Danzig, its main virtue was that "the alternative system is thus backed up by the established system."[5] For the Kpelle, of course, the "alternative" system *was* the established system, a distinction that made all the difference. Unless American courts were suddenly acknowledged as the colonizing institutions of an alien regime (a proposition that surely made sense to ghetto residents, if not to law reformers), anthropological analogies were unlikely to provide solace or solutions for American cities. Tribal models, however enticing, were too rooted in different cultural values for successful transplantation. Harlem was not Liberia.

Disputes, as anthropologists have sensitively demonstrated, are "social processes embedded in social relations." They express personality and culture; they are not disembodied abstractions. It is by now axiomatic among legal anthropologists that "the greater the relational distance between the parties to a dispute, the more likely is law to be used to settle the dispute." Where a community definition of justice (and even honor) prevails, judicial resolution of "private" disputes according to "neutral principles" and due-process guarantees makes no sense. It contradicts the fundamental shared assumptions of participants, for whom disputes are not private, principles are not neutral, and due process is an impediment. In a tribal, village, or rural context, the threat of outside intervention usually suffices to turn disputes inward among the primal social group. Disputants mobilize mediators who are bound to them by shared personal connections and experiences. In modern urban society, however, the community is too fragmented to assert control over the conflict. Strangers, often with "nothing more in common than the dispute itself," must turn to law. Courts, however, care little for the social setting of conflict. They empty a dispute of its social content: as a dispute becomes a case, "it must be translated from social language into legal language." Court intervention is most appropriate in a setting where conflict occurs among unequal strangers, when a court can, at least in theory, rectify an imbalance by extending the formalities of equal protection to weaker parties. Where courts prevail, however, mediation collapses into little more than a preliminary stage in legal proceedings, controlled by court personnel and dependent for its success upon the threat of judicial sanctions. Once the fundamental attributes of social cohesion are missing, the substance of mediation has been transformed, though its form is unchanged. Then, however, its otherwise benign qualities endanger isolated individuals with minimal resources. The weaker party, denied opportunity for legal redress, will be at an even greater disadvantage as informality compounds inequality. At this point it becomes appropriate to inquire whose interests mediation serves and whether it promotes or retards the ends of justice that its proponents claim to pursue.[6]

The element of urgency that finally institutionalized alternative dispute settlement in the 1970s came from within the legal system itself, where signs of congenital breakdown were abundant. It was widely acknowledged that traditional institutions of conflict resolution (religion, family, community) were debilitated in modern society. Courts had tried to compensate, to no avail. Their procedures, even lawyers conceded, "are ossified to the point, priced to the level, and slow to the degree where they cannot flexibly assist disputants in resolving their everyday disputes." Worried professional observers described a "legal explosion" that spread "legal pollution," as "thickening layers of legalism seem to surround our lives." A "tidal wave of litigation" threatened to engulf the judiciary, where all personal grievances and social issues seemed to be converted into legal claims. Amid "the growing intrusion of law on every aspect of American society" courts were asked to assume a "backbreaking burden" of supervision and regulation for which they were institutionally unsuited. Indeed, they had come to serve "not only as lighthouses for the hopeful, but also as lightning rods for the frustrated." Lawyers agreed that there was "too much law, too little justice," a condition all too likely to elevate popular dissatisfaction with the judicial system to dangerous levels.[7]

Beneath this apprehension about the efficacy of adjudication lurked two converging concerns. One was explicitly political, a conservative effort to restore courts to the abstemious purity of judicial restraint—and to deter them from further encouraging legal change in the interest of disadvantaged groups. The Supreme Court, at least since the *Brown* desegregation decision in 1954, had demonstrated unprecedented sensitivity to the legal rights of disadvantaged citizens, with other federal courts trailing in its activist wake (and occasionally prodding). As courts impeded discrimination based on race, gender, or wealth, a generation of Americans looked to a vigorous, vigilant judiciary to enforce the Bill of Rights. The judiciary developed procedural safeguards in criminal law, protected the rights of the indigent, and expanded the right to counsel. New rules—superseding old notions of who could sue or be sued, and about what—reduced the immunity of public officials and enlarged litigation opportunities for victims of discrimination, harassment, and official lawlessness. Judicial activism in pursuit of egalitarian goals was complemented by various initiatives in the public and private sectors: a new conception of "public-interest" law; a federal legal services program; class-action lawsuits; litigation as an instrument to pry open closed institutions (prisons, schools, hospitals) to public scrutiny and government regulation. Within little more than a decade, legal representation and litigation had been transformed into vital ingredients of social justice in the modern state.

Judicial activism propelled the latent political content of law to the surface of public discourse, where conservatives and legalists least wanted it to be. Their usual (silent) formulation suggested that while law served the status quo it was "neutral"; once it began to promote the redistribution of power it was "political." Not only had the judiciary encouraged the assertion of legal claims in the interest of securing equal rights; judicial activism also thrust courts into a controversial supervisory role within institutions that had defaulted on their obligations to provide for weak, stigmatized, or incarcerated Americans. The more courts filled that "vacuum of effective authority," however, the more they were criticized for overreaching the proper limits of their authority. On the assumption that "the less courts do, the more they can do well," courts were admonished to narrow their jurisdictional range so as not to meddle in social problems (employment discrimination, segregation) with remedies (affirmative action, busing) that carried them beyond their institutional competence.[8] A conservative political backlash stung the judiciary for its aggressive protection of minority rights, equal opportunity, and extension of due-process guarantees.

The complementary concern about the judiciary was more institutional, originating at the mundane level of urban criminal and civil courts, where there were evident signs of crisis. There, the problem was not activism but imminent paralysis. Criminal courts could not begin to satisfy the myth of adversary justice. Indeed, it was calculated that if any significant proportion of criminal cases ever actually went to trial, the administration of justice in American cities would disintegrate altogether. Plea-bargaining barely kept the system afloat, at the cost of an insidious dilemma: if legitimacy depended upon adherence to the legal forms of a fair trial, necessity required their circumvention in order to process the deluge of criminal complaints. In civil proceedings, the problem seemed less acute because negotiated settlements ordinarily concerned money, not liberty. Even there, however, the same litany of deficiencies was endlessly recited: court congestion; delay; high costs; denial of access. As these institutional and political concerns converged, non-legal dispute settlement was prescribed as a remedy.[9]

Support for it among legal professionals, however, slipped quickly into a constricted argument for judicial efficiency. The decisive moment in the legalization of informal alternatives came in 1976, at the National Conference on the Causes of Popular Dissatisfaction with the Administration of Justice. The conference, sponsored by the American Bar Association and assorted judicial organizations, honored Roscoe Pound's memorable ABA address (of the same title) seventy years earlier, which had defined the law-reform agenda for his generation. Conference participants, commemorating Pound's address, repeated his complaints. In a foreword to the conference proceedings, three former ABA presidents warned of a "real and present danger" that "the never-ending demands on the American judicial system may, if there is no relief, so overwhelm the capacity of the courts that people will become disenchanted." Although popular disenchantment was the ostensible subject, professional uneasiness was the prevailing mood. Bar leaders, alarmed by persistent public criticism and low professional esteem after the Watergate scandals, narrowly defined the problem as an overburdened judiciary: a "basically sound mechanism," according to Chief Justice Warren Burger, that required modern streamlining. Court reform was the major preoccupation of participants, who inquired whether too much was asked of courts (yes); whether litigation was too complex (yes); and whether the adversarial system was functioning optimally (no). The persistent cause of the judicial malaise, participants agreed, was "simply overload."[10]

Given these assumptions, the idea of alternative dispute settlement gained credibility as a step toward speedy, flexible justice. The Chief Justice proposed informal neighborhood tribunals for minor claims. Professor Frank Sander of Harvard suggested a dispute-resolution center, where disputants would be channeled by a screening clerk into the appropriate process (arbitration, mediation, ombudsman, litigation). Sander, too, was troubled by the unwieldy share of dispute settlement allocated to courts in a society that seemed to have an infinite capacity to generate new sources of conflict. Courts were overburdened to the point of collapse, he suggested, because they assumed "complex and unorthodox tasks" of social regulation rather than confining their activities to what they were "best suited" to do. If the varieties of dispute processing were multiplied, then courts would be protected from litigants "swamping and paralyzing them with cases that do not require their unique capabilities."[11]

Alternative dispute settlement was an idea whose time had come, but no longer as an instrument of community empowerment. In practice (whether or not by design), it was most enthusiastically prescribed for disadvantaged citizens who only recently had begun to litigate successfully to protect and extend their rights. Alternative processes suddenly became a panacea for the resolution of consumer complaints, prisoners' grievances, problems of juveniles and the elderly, and the claims and disputes of Indians and Eskimos. As a result, citizens disadvantaged in American society by race, class, age, or national origin—those who most needed legal rights and remedies—faced the prospect of reduced possibilities for legal redress, in the name of increased access to justice and judicial efficiency. New mediation programs were designed for a preponderantly low-income, minority-group clientele, confined by race and class to inner-city neighborhoods. Their "minor" disputes were designated as "inappropriate for adjudication"; valuable court time must be reserved for "more appropriate cases." As Chief Justice Burger explained, with conspicuous condescension: "The notion that ordinary people want black-robed judges, well-dressed lawyers, and fine paneled courtrooms as the setting to resolve their disputes is not correct. People with problems, like people with pain, want relief, and they want it as quickly and inexpensively as possible."[12]

Why ordinary people should want, or be entitled to, anything less than the formalities of legalized dispute resolution was not immediately apparent. Evictions and repossessions, after all, were as important to them as securities disputes and anti-trust proceedings were to corporations. The "backlash" point was promptly made at the Pound Conference. As federal judge A. Leon Higginbotham, Jr., reminded conference participants, judicial congestion, so excoriated by lawyers and judges, was one consequence of the "long-overdue expansion of many substantive rights" for the dispossessed: "the black, the weak, the poor, the consumer, and the laborer." Diversion of disputes to alternative forums might indeed lighten the judicial burden; but it would do so at the risk of transforming powerless people "into victims who can secure relief neither in the courts nor anywhere else." Legal anthropologist Laura Nader dismissed the effort to divert disputes into neighborhood tribunals as a singularly inappropriate remedy when the very process of legalization had already "sabotaged the community." Solicitor General Wade McCree subsequently warned that neighborhood centers, dispensing informal justice, would seriously disadvantage the "underclass."[13] A day in court would still be reserved for those who could afford the high price of counsel—and justice.

As law reformers rediscovered alternative dispute settlement, however, they prescribed it as a new wonder drug. Consumer grievances attracted a flurry of interest in arbitration. Individualized litigation, slow and costly, seemed hopelessly ill-suited to consumer redress; small-claims courts, the Progressive remedy, had long provided special service to merchants and businessmen who used the courts to pursue default judgments against their debt-ridden customers. But consumer arbitration proposals tended to ignore the fact that in any dispute between customer and company, where economic power was unevenly distributed, informal proceedings ill-served the purchaser. Sales contracts, modeled on commercial arbitration agreements, often required the submission of future disputes to arbitration. Purchasers who did not understand the fine print of their sales contract belatedly discovered that their uninformed consent had deprived them of legal rights. Courts rejected arguments that such arbitration clauses were either unconscionable or that they constituted an unknowing waiver of rights. Diversion of consumer grievances to arbitration not only constricted the scope of judicial review and muffled public disclosure of consumer fraud; it weakened the possibility of effective consumer relief through class-action litigation. Class-action lawsuits enabled individual grievants to aggregate their claims so that one party (representing all purchasers of defective cars or inflammable children's clothing) might sue and recover on behalf of all. But this assertion of consumer power threatened corporate profits. The scope of class-action consumer redress was sharply curtailed by the Supreme Court—and the advocacy of consumer arbitration intensified.[14]

Arbitration for prison inmates and mediation for juvenile offenders developed within a similar framework of backlash against the assertion of legal rights. Just as compulsory consumer arbitration undercut the threat of class-action litigation, alternative processes for prisoners and juveniles diverted grievances after substantial legal victories had been won in court. In the sixties, sparked by momentous Supreme Court decisions in *Gideon*, which extended the right to counsel in criminal proceedings, and *Gault*, which applied due-process protection to juveniles, litigation promised to become an effective weapon for both groups. Prison inmates translated their legal sensitivities into a flood of petitions for expanded due-process rights, which courts began to monitor more attentively than ever before. In response, arbitration of inmate complaints was hailed as "a major breakthrough" that could provide "a quick and definitive resolution" of grievances before they erupted in violence or submerged the courts. Arguably, however, prisoner grievance arbitration served courts better than prisoners. At a time when 5 percent of civil litigation in federal courts involved prisoners'-rights cases, arbitration might lighten the judicial burden. But prisoners faced the prospect of diminished access to precisely those outside institutions which might provide a measure of supervision or protection.[15]

In juvenile proceedings mediation represented one more swing of the reform pendulum toward informality. At the turn of the

century, Progressive experts had argued strenuously and successfully for the removal of juveniles from the court system and for
the development of more benevolent, informal proceedings. By
the sixties, critics perceived the rampant injustices of informal
proceedings, which consigned youngsters to substantial periods
of incarceration without even minimal due-process protection.
With *Gault*, courts began to spin a web of legal protection
around juvenile rights. The compensatory swing in the seventies
to diversion and mediation for juvenile status-offenders blended
some minimal benefits of legality with conspicuous deficiences of
informality. In one "exemplary" pilot project, for example, mediation transpired in "a courtroom-like setting" before a lawyer-
mediator. If the juvenile denied the charge, the case was referred
to court for formal processing; if the juvenile acknowledged
guilt, mediation proceeded (with the offender represented by
counsel). In this setting, mediation hardly was an alternative to
the legal process. It had been refurbished as a coercive form of
juvenile plea-bargaining, with pressure for a guilty plea as the
inducement for diversion to a mediator who determined the appropriate restitution.[16]

As other disadvantaged groups turned to lawyers and courts
for redress, the virtues of informality were also asserted on their
behalf. After legal services were provided to elderly citizens,
enabling them to litigate to secure their rights and benefits,
alternative dispute settlement was hailed as "a timely, inexpensive,
accessible, and humanistic forum" for their grievances. (The
legal system, the argument went, was excessively intimidating, a
proposition belied by the willingness of elderly people to assert
their rights when legal services attorneys were funded to represent them). So, too, in landlord-tenant relations. In the South
Bronx, the most blighted residential area in New York, tenants had
long been victimized by the inequities of judicial proceedings: dis-
possession notices were consigned to "sewer service," depriving
tenants of required warning; judges disregarded procedural re-
quirements for summary evictions; usually only landlords were
represented by counsel. Once legal services attorneys began to

use available legal weapons—especially evidentiary rules and procedural technicalities—to protect tenants and increase their bargaining power, landlords became disenchanted with formal legal proceedings. At the instigation of real-estate interests, a new housing court provided speedy, informal dispute processing within a framework of conciliation. Hearing officers, none of whom lived in the Bronx, replaced judges; suits and plywood tables were substituted for robes and the judicial bench. But the result was that the informal housing tribunal was transformed into a rent-collection and eviction agency (following the small-claims court model); conciliation constricted the legal rights of tenants and erased the protection they had achieved in court from aggressive legal counsel pursuing a strategy of legal formalism.[17]

Nothing, it seemed, propelled enthusiasm for alternative dispute settlement like a few legal victories that unsettled an equilibrium of privilege. Once native Americans litigated to retain tribal lands seized in violation of treaty rights, the federal Bureau of Indian Affairs proclaimed the value of informality. And in Alaska, conciliation proposals were designed to integrate Eskimo tribal justice into the state legal process. There was an especially diabolical quality to prescriptions of informal dispute settlement for native Americans who, for centuries, had practiced their own indigenous tribal forms of dispute settlement—until white intruders imposed the norms of legal adjudication. After the tribes were conquered, and confined within reservations, the rule of law was applied as a double standard. While Indian crimes might be punished according to law, seldom was it possible for Indian claims to be secured in court, where an Indian had no status "except as a criminal." Reservation courts for Indian offenses, established at the instigation of the Bureau of Indian Affairs, were primarily designed for acculturation and control. In time, the government replaced them with tribal courts, which administered tribal codes that occasionally contained "something with Indian roots." The tribal courts, at best, were separate but unequal replicas of white judicial institutions, designed "to make Indians more like white men."[18]

The effort succeeded, with ironic results. A resurgence of "red power" in the sixties prompted Indian-rights litigation to secure dishonored land and resource (especially oil) claims. Despite the tortuousness of its progress through the legal labyrinth, it threatened to remove Indians from their "precariously unprotected state"—and, most ominously, to restore Indian tribal property. That was sufficient to prompt the federal government to reconsider the wisdom of Indian-rights litigation. The Department of the Interior and the Bureau of Indian Affairs admonished Indians to pursue any future disputes with the government through non-judicial means, rather than by litigation. Even their own legal defense organizations suggested that they learn "the rules of these games" to survive in an environment that was increasingly hostile to the assertion of Indian rights. The government thereby trapped Indians in a legal dilemma: it required them to embrace law on the reservations, where mandatory application of constitutional rights and procedural guarantees substantially reduced their tribal autonomy by imposing alien values; and to relinquish law at the courthouse steps, where litigation could enhance their power. Either way, the shifting political currents of legality and informality, applied to native Americans, simultaneously reduced their tribal cohesion and diminished their legal rights.[19]

For Eskimos, too, the process of legalization and cultural subversion dated from expanded white settler contact with natives. At the turn of the century missionaries had introduced village councils to replace traditional men's houses, where Eskimo elders collectively resolved conflict in the interest of tribal harmony. The councils, although compelled to take notice of legal rules, relegated law to the periphery whenever possible, encouraging a form of indigenous "bush justice" to flourish until statehood. Then a concerted effort was made to absorb the Eskimos within the Alaska legal system. The Chief Justice of the Alaska courts advocated "reforms in rural justice"; a conference on bush justice endorsed local dispute-settlement procedures only if they were "extensions of the court system"; villagers were instructed that informality and "summary justice" violated the norms of due process; magistrates' courts encroached upon the village councils. By 1970, as a consequence, "village justice was on the verge of collapse," crippled by alien legal forms that weakened tribal processes. At that point, new conciliation procedures were introduced to integrate tribal practice into the Alaska state justice system.[20] The Eskimos were left to assert their own decimated cultural values within alien legal institutions.

Urban mediation programs often displayed similar insensitivity to local mores. Their inner-city targets were least likely to possess those attributes of community which, historically, had sustained non-legal dispute settlement. For precisely that reason, however, they were most likely to be selected as pilot projects for experiments designed to alleviate the inadequacies of overburdened municipal courts, to reduce the danger of social conflict, and, if possible, to restore some missing ingredients of communal cohesion. The Pound Conference Follow-Up Task Force had advocated neighborhood centers as "new mechanisms for the delivery of justice." The model project, a night prosecutor program established in Columbus, Ohio, in 1971, was solidly entrenched in the criminal justice system. whose interests it served. Interpersonal disputes and minor criminal charges, usually between disputants with a continuing and troubled relationship, were diverted to mediation for resolution by local law students. The program depended entirely upon support from the police, the prosecutor's office, and the courts; its caseload was shaped primarily by considerations of prosecutorial efficiency. Its purpose, the Department of Justice noted approvingly, was "*not* to remove the spectre of 'the long arm of the law' from the process of dispute settlement." Indeed, that long arm was evident in the location of hearings in police headquarters near court and jail, reminding disputants that the project was "a legitimate part of the criminal justice system."[21]

The Justice Department, in fact, conceded that existing alternative projects (those in Philadelphia, Columbus, Dorchester, Miami, and Cincinnati pre-dated the Pound Conference) were "essentially extensions of the courts with which they were affiliated. . . . Very few dispute settlement programs rely heavily on cases generated from the community itself." Close ties to criminal justice agencies guaranteed a supply of referrals, assured legal supervision of the dispute-resolution process, and made "requests" for the appearance of disputants "very persuasive." The usual notice, on official stationary, reminded disputants that failure to appear for mediation might result in the filing of criminal charges. "Subtle forms of coercive pressure," noted an interim Justice Department report, "are important elements in the building of sizeable caseloads."[22]

The new neighborhood justice centers, a response to Pound Conference proposals, opened in Atlanta, Kansas City, and Los Angeles during 1978. They were sponsored by the Department of Justice and securely located within the judicial system. The Atlanta and Kansas City centers functioned in the shadow of the local courts. Most referrals came from judges and prosecutors; relations with court officials were "carefully cultivated." These relationships determined the identity of disputants and the nature of their disputes, for the cases consigned to mediation were those that the courts wished to divert. The disputants were disproportionately female, black or Hispanic, and poor; their disputes were with each other (involving domestic disagreements and neighborly nuisances), not with organizations or businesses. Only the Los Angeles project, sponsored by the local bar association, achieved a measure of independence from the courts. But, located amid a transient population in a multi-ethnic neighborhood "without common goals and values," it rested on a precarious community base. Whether the new justice centers turned toward, or away from, the courts, they faced the impossible task of combining community autonomy with judicial control.[23]

Wherever new dispute-settlement institutions sprouted in the seventies, lawyers were conspicuous and local residents were conspicuously silent. "Trial by lawyer," not trial by jury, was becoming the pervasive mode. Small-claims arbitration was conducted before three-lawyer panels in Pennsylvania. Arbitration by lawyers constituted part of a court reorganization plan in New York, where private law offices served as small-claims courtrooms. In Florida, a "citizen dispute settlement" mediation program referred disputes to panels of volunteer attorneys. In California, the most prominent feature of a small-claims court in a largely Mexican-American neighborhood of San Jose was the presence of lawyers, nominated by the local bar association and appointed by the courts as mediators and arbitrators. Bench and bar were appropriately supportive. Judges were delighted with the prospect of reduced caseloads; lawyers complimented each other for promoting "good public relations" at a time of low professional esteem after Watergate. A streamlined judiciary, supplemented by efficient dispute-settlement procedures outside the courtroom (but not too far from the courthouse), pleased the Chief Justice, the Attorney General, and the bar associations and judicial conferences that enthusiastically endorsed the new reform.[24] If the key to any reform is what it provides to the reformers who propose it, bench and bar clearly had the most to gain from alternative dispute settlement.

There were, as always, unanticipated consequences of the reformers' good intentions. Perhaps the most illuminating (and historically poignant) example was Dorchester, the largest neighborhood in metropolitan Boston. It contained the standard urban volatile mix of established middle-class whites, hostile to a massive influx of impoverished black and Hispanic newcomers. In Dorchester, by the late sixties, these "striking and undoubtedly provocative disparities" had erupted into overt hostility that threatened to engulf the judiciary, whose tasks of dispute settlement were compounded by the most rapidly accelerating crime rate of any neighborhood in metropolitan Boston. Dorchester was located not far from Dedham and Sudbury, its seventeenth-century forebears in the development of non-legal dispute settlement, but there was little to connect their respective experiments. A new urban court mediation program—an alternative to criminal prosecution for family and neighborhood disputes—was designed for Dorchester. If it could build "a human connection" between defendant, victim, and community, it might change "a busy and mechanical urban court into an institution that would provide justice in human terms, as a healing and reconciling experience." One enthusiastic preliminary assessment suggested that "there may be in the rich, 'participatory' symbolism of community mediation the seeds for the growth of a new ethos of cultural values," an ethos rooted in harmony and consensus rather than in disruptive conflict.[25]

According to early evaluations, the Dorchester program successfully resolved varied interpersonal conflicts that involved minor assaults and harassment between neighbors, friends, and family members. Disputants responded positively; they attributed substantial improvement in their situations to mediation, expressing considerable satisfaction with the mediators, who were all Dorchester residents, for their empathetic listening and support. As more evidence accumulated, however, it suggested that the new urban court, ostensibly designed as an alternative to adjudication, actually functioned as a lesser adjunct of the local district court, from which it received nearly all of its referrals. Indeed, the two courts represented competing interests in Dorchester. The law reformers who founded the urban court were committed to active community participation in dispute-settlement processes that would heal and reconcile, not isolate and punish. But the presiding judge of the district court, expressing strong reservations about involving lay citizens in dispute settlement, preferred mediation to serve the efficiency needs of his own tribunal. By controlling the diversion of cases to mediation, and deterring self-generated cases, district court personnel deprived the mediation tribunal of an independent existence. "Community" mediation was absorbed by adjudication. Despite high neighborhood visibility, approval, and cost-free services, Dorchester residents only four times in two years sought mediation on their own initiative. The most striking feature of the new mediation process (in neighborhood justice centers as in Dorchester) was its inability to attract disputes independent of referrals from the judicial system. With the presiding district court judge apprehensive lest judicial control be compromised by deflections from his own court, mediation slipped into the institutional cracks between the "community" proclaimed by reformers and the adjudicatory power of the local judge.[26]

The fragility of the Dorchester community empowered the local district court and undercut mediation as an alternative. In an atomistic social environment, only the court possessed sufficient coercive power to secure the compliance of disputing parties. Mediation was an unfamiliar process in Dorchester. Mediators, although local residents, were "strangers with unknown values." Above all, mediation required a social context of intimacy, reciprocity, and permanence that was conspicuously missing in Dorchester, as in other American urban neighborhoods. The choice of forum, in Dorchester as elsewhere, reflected the degree of neighborhood cohesion. In a Boston inner-city neighborhood near Dorchester, for example, black and white residents, lacking a sustaining network of community supports, readily took their disputes to court; while their Chinese neighbors, who depended upon community relationships for employment and social interaction, went to court with considerable reluctance. Dorchester and Dedham were only miles apart, but the possibilities for communal dispute settlement without law, so evident in the seventeenth century, were all but obliterated in the twentieth. Alternative dispute settlement served as a tenacious metaphor for missing elements of community in American cities, but there was little in urban life to sustain it as a functioning process. All signs pointed to the same conclusion about urban justice: "Life rather than logic makes self-referred mediation as unpalatable to Americans as it is attractive to the peoples of other cultures."[27]

The new urban mediation alternatives contradicted virtually every prerequisite for informal justice that comparative anthropology and American history provided. Communities played no role in their design or implementation. The site-selection process suggested that community fragmentation, not community cohesion, was the primary criterion. Rochester, Dorchester, and Harlem, to cite three early recipients of mediation programs, all had recently experienced acute tension and overt conflict—and, significantly, signs of incipient political activism among community residents, which government officials and legal professionals preferred to stifle, through formal or informal means. Legal institutions hovered over the new mediation programs; virtually every project, by design, received the overwhelming preponderance of its referrals from criminal justice agencies. With legal coercion permeating the mediation process, few neighbors brought their disputes to neighborhood justice centers.[28] An indigenous community practice had come to serve the interests of the state legal system in promoting the efficient processing of criminal complaints.

The arguments for alternative dispute settlement rested on the demonstrable proposition that courts could not effectively resolve the nagging small disputes of people who were involved in continuing relationships. As a neutral statement of fact, oblivious to social class, that certainly was correct. But the new mediation proposals were not oblivious to social class. The poverty line largely determined their clientele. As identifiable groups of citizens, mostly poor and black, were diverted to informal institutions, the danger that they would lose access to courts, and the opportunity for redress there, moved closer to reality. The multiplication of mediation centers made access to justice more difficult, not less, by directing people to "exit points" from judicial institutions. Those who were likely to fare poorly in court were unlikely to receive substantial protection from informal proceedings. The longer the reach of informal processes the likelier it was that certain disputes (perhaps trivial at the level of an individual grievance but with potentially broad political and social implications for all victims of discrimination if adjudicated) might be excluded from the courts altogether. In the end, the justice system was the "community" that the new mediation programs most effectively represented.[29]

Justice centers and their progeny managed to combine some of the worst features of legality *and* of informality, without incorporating many advantages of either. Government sponsorship encouraged the extension of state legal control into urban neighborhoods, bringing private disputes under official scrutiny. At the same time, however, mediation processes dispensed with due-process safeguards (representation by counsel and the right to a jury trial), making rights even more precarious than they were in court without compensatory benefits to disputants. With relatively little at stake in any particular dispute, mediation tribunals could encourage procedural flexibility "and present the result as fair compromise." But compromise only is an equitable solution between equals; between unequals, it "inevitably reproduces inequality." Alternative dispute settlement offered mechanical remedies for political problems: the characteristic response of law reformers since the turn of the century as they struggled to neutralize political opposition to the values that the legal system protected.[30]

Today alternative dispute settlement, without sustenance from sources independent of the legal system, drifts aimlessly. The appropriate monument to its current paralysis as an effective expression of community empowerment is the Dispute Resolution Act of 1980. In a series of sweeping declarations that echoed Roscoe Pound's complaints seventy-five years earlier, Congress concluded that for most Americans mechanisms for the resolution of "minor" disputes were "largely unavailable, inaccessible, ineffective, expensive, or unfair." These disputes, in the aggregate, were of "enormous social and economic consequence," requiring community-based procedures involving people outside the formal justice system for effective resolution. As a remedy, however, Congress offered little more than a formal gesture of endorsement for a process of dispute settlement that was inappropriate, if not invidious. Even so, not a dollar has yet been expended to implement the purposes of the legislation: to provide access to "community based dispute resolution mechanisms . . . which are effective, fair, inexpensive, and judicious."[81] The Dispute Resolution Act was a hollow shell; it was, therefore, an appropriate symbol of the futile effort to establish justice without law, by law.

Conclusion

Litigation may become a predictable stage in the life-cycle of Americans. Now that children sue their parents, and non-divorcing spouses sue each other, the possibilities are limitless. Parishioners have already sued priests and, appropriately, district attorneys have sued judges. Not long ago a group of parents litigated the error of a football official, winning a judgment in favor of their high school team before the state supreme court overruled it (and, mercifully, a federal judge refused to hear the appeal). "I wish [the parents] would look at what they're doing to our kids," the football coach complained.[1] Like the coach, however, the parents may only have been preparing their children to become good Americans, by demonstrating that the values associated with competitive athletics can be sublimated in adulthood and expressed in litigation. Aggressive struggle, within a highly structured framework of rules, in pursuit of territory and victory, is the ultimate national pastime—in law as in football.

Law has absorbed and strengthened the competitive, acquisitive values associated with American individualism and capitalism. These were, of course, precisely the values that served as negative inspiration for the most daring experiments with non-legal forms of dispute settlement. But legalization and delegalization are processes, not final choices; they move symbiotically, responding to the special circumstances of time, place, and political priorities. As with a child's see-saw, the instant of ascent assures the inevitability of descent. Communal ideals and individual aspirations are in constant flux; disputing patterns help to monitor their relative strength. The rejection of formal legal institutions in American history has been recurrent and purposeful, for law inhibited the reciprocal access and trust cultivated by communities as disparate as Dedham, Oneida, Chinatown, and the Chamber of Commerce. Communal dispute-settlement alternatives were designed to absorb private antagonism in a way that softened the pursuit of individual advantage, transforming it into a source of community strength.

Even in the most committed utopian ventures, however, the flight from legal formality always has remained problematic for Americans. In the American context it seemed quite natural, with the Mayflower Compact as the model, to create utopia by contract. A persistent thread of contractualism ran through the covenanted communities of New England. Two centuries later, utopian constitutions often read like legal charters; utopian boundaries might be constricted by the very legal principles that their members tried with such determination to elude. These anomalous communities relied upon legal instruments to establish alternatives to law. (Now we witness the inverse anomaly: legal professionals tumble over each other in their enthusiasm for non-legal dispute-settlement alternatives.) The proliferation of formal contractual relations, even within utopian communities, is characteristically American. In legal theory contract may express trust, but in social reality our fondness for contract demonstrates a degree of mistrust among people who persistently pursue their own advantage at each other's expense.[2]

With even the most utopian communities tinged with legalism at their inception, the pervasive legalization of alternatives in the modern era is hardly surprising. This is part of a larger transformation in American society that dates at least from the end of the nineteenth century. Amid the social dislocations that accompanied the rapid concentration of wealth and power in the age of industrial expansion, the full force of law was asserted to protect the new social order. Competing pockets of autonomous authority (originating in tribalism, religion, national origin, or class) were suppressed in the interest of nationalism, secularism, and corporate capitalism. Indians were restricted to reservations; Mormonism was confined to its church; immigrants were Americanized; workers were consigned to factory subservience. They all were stripped of dispute-settlement processes that had preserved their internal cohesion but now threatened the legal supremacy of the state. As law expanded its protection of liberty (of contract) and (corporate) property, it relentlessly stifled alternatives. An increasingly formal, professionalized process undercut indigenous systems of dispute settlement, forcing them to accommodate to the dominant legal mode.

Within the legalization process, however, persistent contradictions remained. They recur in every generation to tantalize and frustrate law reformers (now a mixed group of liberal law teachers and conservative judges), for they are as intractable as they are irrepressible. At their core lies the paradox that the more elaborate and sophisticated our legal culture, the more serious is the problem of access to justice. A striking feature of indigenous community dispute settlement, not only in the American experience but in the various cultures that still nourish it, is the virtually total absence of access to justice as a problematic issue. The consuming concern of modern American society with justice simply is not replicated elsewhere. Americans may prefer to believe that this testifies to their own refined and commendable sensitivities; but in fact our preoccupation is only commensurate with the vast array of justice problems that our particular social and legal systems produce. Where the sense of justice is indwelling, integral to the very process of community creation and preservation, access to justice is not a scarce commodity. Once the bonds of community slacken, however, and the meaning of justice collapses into formal legal procedures, justice problems abound.

Then the issues that nag relentlessly at legal institutions begin to intrude. Will additional doses of legalization, in the form of more laws, lawyers, courts, and judges, help or hinder access to justice? Are informal processes necessary, either to soften the rigidities of legal formalism or to reduce the burden on legal institutions? Should legal professionals share their monopoly of dispute-settlement power with lay citizens? Is the public interest served by diversion of disputes to informal institutions, which may assure efficient processing but will surely jeopardize legal rights? Should disputants be encouraged to resolve their conflicts without lawyers, or should they be assured legal services (which not only protect their rights but further contribute to the problem of institutional overload)? These questions converge into more fundamental inquiries about the possibilities of justice within a legalized setting where, by definition, justice has indeterminate meaning. If law effectively protects individual rights—an article of faith among its champions—why is there such persistent pressure (especially from them) for alternative processes? If alternatives are necessary, however, why should they be hitched to the very legal system whose deficiencies create the need for them? After a century of struggle with these issues, legal institutions still demonstrate their incapacity to resolve them within their own premises and procedures. The reasons for this failure lie in cultural values and in social structure.

The dependence of Americans upon law, and their apprehension about it, are reciprocal. The exercise of freedom, channeled into the acquisitive pursuit of wealth, requires the vigorous assertion of individual rights, which law protects. It also assures incessant conflict between competing individuals, who are virtually unrestrained by any purpose beyond self-aggrandizement. The Darwinian jungle is filled with the excitement of the hunt, but it is a scary place because the hunters simultaneously are hunted. As Americans pursue their quarry, they need protection (provided by law) for themselves, and weapons (also provided by law) against their adversaries. So we are possessed of vastly more laws and lawyers than any other society; we are also more concerned with lawlessness than any other people. The more laws we have, of course, the more laws will be broken; the more we then need the services of lawyers and courts; the more congested the legal system becomes; the more we yearn for alternatives; but the less they are able to survive independently of legal institutions.

The legal system now struggles, without appreciable success, to unravel these contradictions before it is choked by them. The current enthusiasm for delegalization represents an effort by legal professionals to put their system back together again. Like the king's horses and men, however, they are overwhelmed by the enormity, indeed the impossibility, of the task. By now, alternative dispute settlement primarily expresses the values of these professionals, who are reluctant to relinquish their control over the disputing process. Their rationale constantly sputters into the same arguments for judicial efficiency that have been heard in legal circles since the turn of the century. Consequently, just when alternative processes seem maximally energetic, they are more derivative and constricted than ever before. With the community impulse so thoroughly commercialized and legalized it could hardly be otherwise.

Law is always more than rules and procedures, statutes and precedents, or courts and lawyers. It is, ultimately, an ideology, a set of beliefs and a system of integrated values that provide elements of predictability, stability, and coherence. Legal institutions, despite their state monopoly, must constantly prove themselves. Legitimacy remains a persistent problem in modern society, which even the rule of law can never entirely resolve. The legitimacy dilemma is inherent: law, designed to protect the propertied Haves, must also validate itself to the disadvantaged Have-Nots. The singular achievement of eighteenth-century English criminal law, as Douglas Hay has shown, was that it enabled English rulers "to make the courts a selective instrument of class justice, yet simultaneously to proclaim the law's incorruptible impartiality." It succeeded by combining the majesty of spectacle and ritual with a sufficient infusion of formal equality to provide the essential minimum of justice. Majesty and justice (with a dose of mercy) elevated English law, "the creature of the ruling class," into "a power with its own claims," even though it was "nine-tenths concerned with upholding a radical division of property."[3]

American legal institutions confront a similar task: to legitimate their rule to all despite their special service to the privileged few. Majesty no longer is a solution. By now, Americans have minimal expectations of it from their legal institutions, and they are seldom disappointed. The wigs and robes of English barristers may still evoke occasional envy among lawyers, but in our more rambunctious and materialistic society large retainer fees and the promise of partnership long ago replaced them as exalted status symbols. Although the marble temple that houses the Supreme Court remains a venerated national shrine, and even the lowliest judge wears a black robe and sits at an elevated bench to command respect, courts inexorably absorb the values of a wheeling and dealing culture. In the halls of justice, as more than one cynic has observed, justice usually is done in the halls. There "bargaining within the shadow of the law" transpires in a tawdry setting that most closely resembles a commodities exchange.[4]

Justice is less amenable than majesty to persuasive symbolic manipulation. For lawyers and judges, justice inheres in form and process; most of its substantive content receded long ago. So Justice Holmes, admonished by a friend to do justice on the bench, replied that his job was only to play according to the rules. Once the meaning of justice is legalized and formalized, however, the rule of law (as the astute Progressive essayist Herbert Croly understood) means "government by lawyers" conducted "in the interest of litigation." And conceptions of justice that rest almost entirely upon legal procedure, as necessary as they may be in a pluralistic society, still trouble ordinary citizens who have difficulty defining justice but know injustice when they receive it. Throughout the twentieth century, as judges and lawyers have monotonously conceded, legal institutions have defaulted on their obligation to provide justice to all. This is surely because the ideal of equal justice is incompatible with the social realities of unequal wealth, power, and opportunity, which no amount of legal formalism can disguise. In an unequal society, the Haves usually are better served by legal formalism than the Have-Nots, a disparity that creates a persistent legitimacy crisis. As justice fragments into formal procedures and private deals, the austere neutrality of law is constantly eroded by the special protection that its form and substance provide to privileged members of society.[5]

As cynicism about the legal system increases, so does enthusiasm for alternative dispute-settlement institutions. The search for alternatives accelerates, as Richard Abel has suggested, "when some fairly powerful interest is threatened by an increase in the number or magnitude of legal rights."[6] Alternatives are designed to provide a safety valve, to siphon discontent from courts. With the danger of political confrontation reduced, the ruling power of legal institutions is preserved, and the stability of the social system reinforced. Not incidentally, alternatives prevent the use of courts for redistributive purposes in the interest of equality, by consigning the rights of disadvantaged citizens to institutions with minimal power to enforce or protect them. It is, therefore, necessary to beware of the seductive appeal of alternative institutions. They may deflect energy from political organization by groups of people with common grievances; or discourage effective litigation strategies that could provide substantial benefits. They may, in the end, create a two-track justice system that dispenses informal "justice" to poor people with "small" claims and "minor" disputes, who cannot afford legal services, and who are denied access to courts. (Bar associations do not recommend that corporate law firms divert *their* clients to mediation, or that business deductions for legal expenses—a gigantic government subsidy for litigation—be eliminated.) Justice according to law will be reserved for the affluent, hardly a novel development in American history but one that needs little encouragement from the spread of alternative dispute-settlement institutions.

It is social context and political choice that determine whether courts, or alternative institutions, can render justice more or less accessible—and to whom. Both can be discretionary, arbitrary, domineering—and unjust. Law can symbolize justice, or conceal repression. It can reduce exploitation, or facilitate it. It can prohibit the abuse of power, or disguise abuse in procedural forms. It can promote equality, or sustain inequality. Despite the resiliency and power of law, it seems unable to eradicate the tension between legality and justice: even in a society of (legal) equals, some still remain more equal than others. But diversion from the legal system is likely to accentuate that inequality. Without legal power the imbalance between aggrieved individuals and corporations, or government agencies, cannot be redressed. In American society, as Laura Nader has observed, "disputing without the force of law . . . [is] doomed to fail."[7] Instructive examples document the deleterious effect of coerced informality (even if others demonstrate the creative possibilities of indigenous experimentation). Freed slaves after the Civil War and factory workers at the turn of the century, like inner-city poor people now, have all been assigned places in informal proceedings that offer substantially weaker safeguards than law can provide. Legal institutions may not provide equal justice under law, but in a society ruled by law it is their responsibility.

It is chimerical to believe that mediation or arbitration can now accomplish what law seems powerless to achieve. The American deification of individual rights requires an accessible legal system for their protection. Understandably, diminished faith in its capacities will encourage the yearning for alternatives. But the rhetoric of "community" and "justice" should not be permitted to conceal the deterioration of community life and the unraveling of substantive notions of justice that has accompanied its demise. There is every reason why the values that historically are associated with informal justice should remain compelling: especially the preference for trust, harmony, and reciprocity within a communal setting. These are not, however, the values that American society encourages or sustains; in their absence there is no effective alternative to legal institutions.

The quest for community may indeed be "timeless and universal."[8] In this century, however, the communitarian search for justice without law has deteriorated beyond recognition into a stunted off-shoot of the legal system. The historical progression is clear: from community justice without formal legal institutions to the rule of law, all too often without justice. But injustice without law is an even worse possibility, which misguided enthusiasm for alternative dispute settlement now seems likely to encourage. Our legal culture too accurately expresses the individualistic and materialistic values that most Americans deeply cherish to inspire optimism about the imminent restoration of communitarian purpose. For law to be less conspicuous Americans would have to moderate their expansive freedom to compete, to acquire, and to possess, while simultaneously elevating shared responsibilities above individual rights. That is an unlikely prospect unless Americans become, in effect, un-American. Until then, the pursuit of justice without law does incalculable harm to the prospect of equal justice.

The current debate over dispute-settlement procedures is likely to continue. It is part of a larger critical examination of the nature of law in capitalist society and its Sisyphian struggle for legitimacy. Even now, when legal institutions seem most securely in place, there are irrepressible doubts about their capacities. But it is an ominous portent when lawyers and judges become the most conspicuous and outspoken proponents of alternatives. The high priests seldom are the first to detect any waning of faith since they usually are the last to experience it. The rule of law usually inspires celebration, not lamentation, especially among the rulers. Their doubts should remind us that while there is much to celebrate in the rule of law, law remains a terrifying, no less than an inspiring, symbol in the twentieth century. Conjoined with bureaucracy and state, it has demonstrated limitless capacity for evil.

No one anticipated this with more chilling prescience than Franz Kafka. In his ominous parable "Before the Law," a man who still believes that law is accessible to everyone finally learns, at the end of a lifetime of futile waiting, that it never will be accessible to him. And after the trial that by now is the apt metaphor for all that is Kafkaesque in modern society, Joseph K. still waits in vain, an instant before his death, for justice from the unseen judge and the inaccessible high court.[9] Kafka knew. He was, after all, trained in the law.

Notes

INTRODUCTION

1. I should state at the outset that there are certain propositions, currently fashionable in legal scholarship, that do not explicitly engage my attention in this book. First, the assertion that "law" is everywhere, not only in cases and statutes, but wherever there are norms, rules, and procedures. Second, the corollary claim that "alternatives" are nowhere; rather, they are minor variations that resemble adversary disputation more than they are distinguished from it. Third, the consequent rejection of any distinction between "formal" legal institutions and "informal" alternatives. My response to each of these assertions is essentially identical: I know both sides of the argument, which I find diversionary if not arid. As a matter of historical fact, if not contemporary legal thought, the distinction between formal legal institutions and informal alternatives (without lawyers, or judges who are officers of the state) made sense to those who chose one over the other. (I concede, however, that there is all too much evidence that the former are now so random, discretionary, arbitrary, or chaotic that they can hardly be considered as a model for anything that resembles formality. And the alternatives have, indeed, been legalized.) If that distinction now seems blurred, with legal and non-legal categories hopelessly jumbled, that is our current problem. It was not a problem for participants in the historical process that this book analyzes, at least not until the twentieth century, when law eclipsed historical alternatives and cast them in its own constricted image.

2. See Harold J. Berman, *The Interaction of Law and Religion* (Nashville, 1974), 11–14; David Little, *Religion, Order and Law* (New York, 1969), 175, 218–19.

3. Roberto Mangabeira Unger, *Law in Modern Society* (New York, 1976), 62.

4. See Laura Nader and Harry F. Todd, Jr. (eds.), *The Disputing Process —Law in Ten Societies* (New York, 1978), 9–19; James L. Gibbs, "Law and Personality: Signposts for a New Direction," in Nader (ed.), *Law in Culture and Society* (Chicago, 1969), 176–207; Victor H. Li, *Law Without Lawyers* (Boulder, Colo., 1978); Lon L. Fuller, "Mediation—Its Forms and Functions," 44 *So. Cal. L.R.* (1971), 325; Nader, "Styles of Court Procedure: To Make the Balance," in *Law in Culture and Society*, 84–88.

5. The examples are drawn from Jerold S. Auerbach, "A Plague of Lawyers," *Harper's* (October 1976), 37–43. The quote from J. Hector St. John de Crèvecoeur is in his *Letters from an American Farmer* (New York, 1957), 135.

6. 2 *Henry VI*, iv.2; Alexis de Tocqueville, *Democracy in America*, ed. Phillips Bradley, 2 vols. (New York, 1945), I:274–76, 278.

7. Thomas Ehrlich, "Legal Pollution," *New York Times Magazine* (February 8, 1976), 17; Bayliss Manning, "Hyperlexis: Our National Disease," 71 *Northwestern L. R.* (1977), 767–82.

8. Manuel Levine, "The Conciliation Court of Cleveland," 2 *J. Amer. Jud. Soc.* (1918), 10.

9. William H. Simon, "The Ideology of Advocacy: Procedural Justice and Professional Ethics," 1978 *Wisc. L.R.*, 115. Several ideas in this and preceding paragraphs were developed in Jerold S. Auerbach, "Welcome to Litigation," *The New Republic*, 184 (January 17, 1981), 19–21.

10. Jethro K. Lieberman, *The Litigious Society* (New York, 1981). Litigation, according to Lieberman (p. 190), is "the hallmark of a free and just society." For the television blurb, see *New York Times* (February 1, 1982).

11. Stanley Diamond, "The Rule of Law Versus the Order of Custom," in Robert Paul Wolff (ed.), *The Rule of Law* (New York, 1971), 115–44; Unger, *Law in Modern Society*, 54–70.

12. Grant Gilmore, *The Ages of American Law* (New Haven, 1977), iii.

13. Quoted in Martin Buber, *Paths in Utopia* (New York, 1950), 76.

I. "IN BROTHERLY AFFECTION": COLONIAL PATTERNS

1. George Lee Haskins, *Law and Authority in Early Massachusetts* (New York, 1960), 35, 117. See also Charles J. Hilkey, *Legal Development in Colonial Massachusetts, 1630–1686* (New York, 1910), 68; Richard B. Morris, Foreword to George A. Billias (ed.), *Law and Authority in Colonial America* (Barre, Mass., 1965).

2. Lewis A. Coser, *The Functions of Social Conflict* (New York, 1956), 20, 71–80, 102, 151–52; Morton Deutsch, *The Resolution of Conflict* (New Haven, 1973), 9–10, 376.

3. Kenneth A. Lockridge, *A New England Town: The First Hundred Years* (New York, 1970), 4–7; John Demos (ed.), *Remarkable Providences: 1600–1760* (New York, 1972), 14–15; Thomas Bender, *Community and Social Change in America* (New Brunswick, 1978), 63–65; Winthrop's sermon is in Perry Miller and Thomas Johnson (eds.), *The Puritans*, 2 vols. (New York, 1963), I:198.

4. William E. Nelson, "The Larger Context of Litigation in Plymouth County, 1725–1825," in David T. Konig (ed.), *Plymouth Court Records, 1686–1859* (Wilmington, Del., 1978), 28.

5. Nelson, "Larger Context," 127–28; Michael Zuckerman, *Peaceable Kingdoms: New England Towns in the Eighteenth Century* (New York, 1970), 47–50, 147–48; David T. Konig, *Law and Society in Puritan Massachusetts* (Chapel Hill, 1979), 136–38. Intense localism also retarded legal development. As town-dwellers turned their energies inward, arbitration and mediation became effective deterrents to the meddling reach of colonial magistrates. See especially T. H. Breen, *Puritans and Adventurers* (New York, 1980), 15–18.

6. John Demos, *A Little Commonwealth: Family Life in Plymouth Colony* (New York, 1970), 9; Nelson, "The Larger Context," 11, 21–33; Emil Oberholzer, Jr., *Delinquent Saints* (New York, 1956), 10, 32–34, 135, 188–89; Haskins, *Law and Authority in Early Massachusetts*, 89–90; Darrett B. Rutman, *Winthrop's Boston: Portrait of a Puritan Town, 1630–1649* (Chapel Hill, 1965), 154–55; M. P. Baumgartner, "Law and Social Status in Colonial New Haven, 1639–1665," 1 *Research in Law and Sociology* (1978), 154–55; Demos, *Remarkable Providences*, 222–39, for a partial transcript of the proceedings; Demos, "Hibbens Case" (unpublished ms., n.d.).

7. Oberholzer, *Delinquent Saints*, 33–35; Nelson, "The Larger Context," 29–31; Demos, *Remarkable Providences*, 238. Mrs. Hibbens fared better in court, where she received a favorable verdict on the original issue of the alleged overcharge. Demos, "Hibbens Case."

8. Lockridge, *New England Town*, 5–6, 13–14, 17–19, 21, 51, 78–79.

9. Sumner Chilton Powell, *Puritan Village* (Middletown, Conn., 1963), 6–11, 10–17, 59, 93–95.

10. *Ibid.*, 98, 107–8, 111–12.

11. Rutman, *Winthrop's Boston*, 154–55, 233–34.

12. Francis R. Aumann, *The Changing American Legal System* (Columbus, 1940), 48–49; Frances Kellor, *Arbitration and the Legal Profession* (New York, 1952), 11–14; Richard B. Morris, *Studies in the History of American Law* (New York, 1930), 42–47, 60–61; "Early American Arbitration: I. An Immigrant in Connecticut," 1 *Arb. J. N.S.* (Spring 1946), 51–54; "Early American Arbitration: II. In Old Virginia," 1 *Arb. J. N.S.* (Summer 1946), 174–76; Gerald W. Gawalt, "Sources of Anti-Lawyer Sentiment in Massachusetts, 1740–1840," 14 *American J. Legal Hist.* (1970), 283–307.

Scattered evidence from southern colonies suggests, by the eighteenth
century, a general pattern of litigiousness with pockets of resistance, especially within Baptist congregational communities. See Wesley Frank Craven,
The Southern Colonies in the Seventeenth Century, 1607–1689 (Baton
Rouge, 1949), 286–87; William Eddis, *Letters from America*, ed. Aubrey C.
Land (Cambridge, Mass., 1969), 64; Richard Beeman, "Social Change and
Cultural Conflict in Virginia: Lunenberg County, 1746 to 1774," 35 *Wm.
and Mary Q.* (July 1978), 470. Professor Kathryn Preyer kindly called my
attention to the last two items. T. H. Breen, in *Puritans and Adventurers*
(xii–xiv, 109–15), has contrasted the corporate insularity of Massachusetts
towns with the fierce competitive individualism of Virginians. It would be
interesting to compare litigation rates in these colonies with this contrast in
mind. For Virginia developments, see A. G. Roeber, *Faithful Magistrates
and Republican Lawyers* (Chapel Hill, 1981).

13. Ezra Michener, *A Retrospect of Early Quakerism* (Philadelphia,
1860), 266–67, 280; George S. Odiorne, "Arbitration and Mediation Among
the Early Quakers," 9 *Arb. J.* (1954), 161–62. See also Thomas Clarkson,
A Portraiture of Quakerism, 3 vols. (London, 1806), II:79–80. Quaker
non-legal dispute settlement was one of many Quaker customs described
by Clarkson as "peculiar."

14. Rufus M. Jones, *The Quakers in the American Colonies* (London,
1911), 141; Odiorne, "Arbitration and Mediation," 162–63; Frederick B.
Tolles, *Meeting House and Counting House* (New York, 1963), 4–8.

15. Michener, *Retrospect*, 269–71; Tolles, *Meeting House and Counting
House*, 251–52. For a hostile interpretation of Quaker antilegalism, see
Daniel J. Boorstin, *The Americans: The Colonial Experience* (New York,
1958), 68. Boorstin, trained as a lawyer, finds it odd that Quakers preferred
arbitration to litigation.

16. H. Clay Reed and George J. Miller (eds.), *The Burlington Court
Book: A Record of Quaker Jurisprudence in West New Jersey, 1680–1709*
(Washington, D.C., 1944), xi.

17. Tolles, *Meeting House and Counting House*, 64–65, 75–76; Odiorne,
"Arbitration and Mediation," 164–65; Reed and Miller, *Burlington Court
Book*, xii, xlvii, 2, 29, 39, 44, 46, 70, 299, 339.

18. *Ibid.*, xlii; Michener, *Retrospect*, 269; J. William Frost, *The Quaker
Family in Colonial America* (New York, 1973), 57.

19. John R. Aiken, "New Netherlands Arbitration in the Seventeenth
Century," 29 *Arb. J.* (1974), 145–60; Bender, *Community and Social Change*,
69–70 (Bender refers aptly to the "subcultural particularism" of the Dutch);
Herbert Alan Johnson, "The Advent of Common Law in Colonial New
York," in Billias (ed.), *Law and Authority in Colonial New York*, 74, 82;
Milton M. Klein, "From Community to Status: The Development of the
Legal Profession in Colonial New York," *New York History*, 60 (April

1979), 133–56; Sabra A. Jones, "Historical Development of Commercial Arbitration in the United States," 12 *Minn. L.R.* (1928), 246–47; Richard B. Morris (ed.), *Select Cases of the Mayor's Court of New York City, 1674–1784* (Washington, D.C., 1935), 44; Morris, "The New York City Mayor's Court," in Leo Hershkowitz and Milton M. Klein (eds.), *Courts and Law in Early New York* (New York, 1978), 21; Berthold Fernow (ed.), *Records of New Amsterdam from 1653 to 1674*, 7 vols. (New York, 1897), I:54, 77, 109, 161, 176, 203; II:53; V:96–97; VI:286–87.

20. Michael Kammen, *Colonial New York* (New York, 1975), 37–41, 47, 55.

21. Earl S. Wolaver, "The Historical Background of Commercial Arbitration," 83 *U. Pa. L.R.* (1934), 132–38, 144–45; James B. Boskey, "A History of Commercial Arbitration in New Jersey," 8 *Rutgers-Camden L.J.* (1976), 1–3; Jones, "Historical Development of Commercial Arbitration," 246–47. For an exploration of merchants' common economic interests, amid social differences, see Bernard Bailyn, *New England Merchants in the Seventeenth Century* (Cambridge, Mass., 1955), 189–97.

22. For late-eighteenth-century patterns, see Morton J. Horwitz, *The Transformation of American Law, 1780–1860* (Cambridge, Mass., 1977), 146–50, 165–67.

23. Charles T. Gwynne, "The Oldest American Tribunal," 1 *Arb. J.* (April 1937), 117; Chamber of Commerce of the State of New York, *Earliest Arbitration Records: Committee Minutes, 1779–1792* (New York, 1928), 4–5, 14–15; William Catron Jones, "Three Centuries of Commercial Arbitration in New York: A Brief Survey," 5 *Wash. U. L.Q.* (1956), 201–6.

24. Honestus [Benjamin Austin], "Observations on the Pernicious Practice of the Law" (Boston, 1819), reprinted in 13 *American J. Legal Hist.* (1969), 244–302.

25. John H. Murrin, "Review Essay," 11 *History and Theory* (1972), 248–51. See also L. Kinvin Wroth, "Possible Kingdoms: The New England Town from the Perspective of Legal History," 15 *American J. Legal Hist.* (1971), 318–30; David G. Allen, "The Zuckerman Thesis and the Process of Legal Rationalization in Provincial Massachusetts," 29 *Wm. and Mary Q.* (1972), 443–60; Konig, *Law and Society*, 43–48, 76–81, 88, 107, 188–91.

26. Rutman, *Winthrop's Boston*, 234, 239, 249–51, 277; John H. Murrin, "The Legal Transformation: The Bench and Bar of Eighteenth-Century Massachusetts," in Stanley N. Katz (ed.), *Colonial America* (Boston, 1971), 417–21; James A. Henretta, "Economic Development and Social Structure in Colonial Boston," in *ibid.*, 450–51; Powell, *Puritan Village*, 96–97, 118, 121–25, 131–32, 140, 145. For analysis of a similar pattern in Andover, another open-field village, see Philip J. Greven, Jr., *Four Generations* (Ithaca, 1970). Even so, communal ideology persisted until well into the eighteenth

century, as suggested in Robert A. Gross, *The Minutemen and Their World* (New York, 1976).

27. Lockridge, *New England Town*, 85, 91, 145, 159.

28. William Bradford, *Of Plymouth Plantation*, ed. Samuel Eliot Morison (New York, 1967), 75–76, 120–21, 333–34.

29. Nelson, "The Larger Context," 52–55, 61–65, 128.

30. *Ibid.*, 11, 15–16, 24–26, 30–31, 55, 126–32; Demos, *A Little Commonwealth*, 49. Demos offers the intriguing, if undocumentable, suggestion that the price of domestic peace within crowded family quarters was the displacement of anger and aggression from family members to neighbors. To keep smiling at their family members, people sued their neighbors (50–51).

31. Paul Boyer and Stephen Nissenbaum, *Salem Possessed* (Cambridge, Mass., 1974), 6–7, 45, 51, 86–89; Konig, *Law and Society*, 64–116.

32. *Ibid.*, 65, 78–88, 91–92, 107, 108, 112, 116. If Lockridge makes the most compelling argument, in the seventeenth-century American context, for the emergence of the rule of law as a measure of the decline of community, Konig makes the strongest case for the integrative, community-binding function of legalization. Far more striking than their disagreement over the meaning of change, however, is their agreement on the nature of change and the replacement of a social order based on custom with one based on the rule of law. The momentum, as Konig suggests, was "from communalism to litigation" (ch. 4); the rising incidence of litigation can be read to measure the decline of communitarian coherence *and* the assertion of an integrative impulse through law.

33. Konig, *Law and Society*, 158–80; Boyer and Nissenbaum, *Salem Possessed*, 2–7, 23–26, 103–7. It is revealing that even when Salem ministers applied pressure to halt the trials, their opposition was expressed in evidentiary (i.e. legalistic) terms (9–11).

34. See especially Keith Thomas, *Religion and the Decline of Magic* (New York, 1971), 556–67.

35. Alan Macfarlane, *Witchcraft in Tudor and Stuart England* (New York, 1970), 192–206; Thomas, *Religion and the Decline of Magic*, 560–61; John Demos, "Underlying Themes in the Witchcraft of Seventeenth Century New England," 75 *American Hist. R.* (1970), 1311–26; Konig, *Law and Society*, 146–57, 170–75.

36. David G. Allen, *In English Ways* (Chapel Hill, 1981), 237–41. For this pattern in Connecticut, see Richard L. Bushman, *From Puritan to Yankee* (New York, 1970), 37–38, 56–60, 72, 82.

37. Bushman, *From Puritan to Yankee*, 184–85, 193–94; Alan Heimert, *Religion and the American Mind* (Cambridge, Mass., 1966), 180–82.

38. Bushman, *From Puritan to Yankee*, 231–35; Nelson, "The Larger Context," 120–23; Oberholzer, *Delinquent Saints*, 239.

39. Heimert, *Religion and the American Mind*, 181–82; William E. Nelson, *Americanization of the Common Law* (Cambridge, Mass., 1975), 4, 115–16, 143, 174.

40. See Richard D. Brown, *Modernization: The Transformation of American Life, 1600–1865* (New York, 1976), 56–59.

41. See Robert Redfield, *The Little Community* (Uppsala, 1955), 108–10; Bender, *Community and Social Change*, 6–11, 118, 146–47.

42. Horwitz, *The Transformation of American Law*, 154–55.

43. Thomas, *Religion and the Decline of Magic*, 526–28.

44. Cited in Page Smith, *As a City Upon a Hill* (New York, 1966), 132. Smith distinguishes between covenanted and cumulative communities: the former were characterized by mutual bonds of faith, structure, and order; the latter by the random gathering of assorted, unconnected individuals. Non-legal and legal patterns of dispute settlement seem to have corresponded with this division.

II. THE DIVIDED LEGACY: FROM BIBLE COMMUNISM TO INDUSTRIAL COMMONWEALTH

1. L. F. Greene (ed.), *The Writings of the Late Elder John Leland* (New York, 1845), 292. The other quotations are drawn from the following titles: Roscoe Pound, *The Formative Era of American Law* (Boston, 1938); Charles M. Haar (ed.), *The Golden Age of American Law* (New York, 1965); Morton J. Horwitz, *The Transformation of American Law* (Cambridge, Mass., 1977). For New England, see William E. Nelson, *Dispute and Conflict Resolution in Plymouth County, Massachusetts, 1725–1825* (Chapel Hill, 1981), 134–42. For the frontier, see Elizabeth Gaspar Brown, "Frontier Justice: Wayne County, 1796–1836," 16 *American J. Legal Hist.* (1972), 152. For revivalism, see Perry Miller, *The Life of the Mind in America* (New York, 1965), 19, 70. But for the retention of church dispute settlement on the frontier, especially among Presbyterians, Baptists, and Methodists, see T. Scott Miyakowa, *Protestants and Pioneers* (Chicago, 1964), 23, 38, 55. Among these religious groups litigation was anathema; church discipline and arbitration were preferred.

2. William Duane, *Sampson Against the Philistines, or The Reformation of Lawsuits* (Philadelphia, 1805), iii–iv, 24–25, 29, 32–36, 38, 66, 68–69, 96.

3. Richard E. Ellis, *The Jeffersonian Crisis: Courts and Politics in the Young Republic* (New York, 1971), 200–201, 255; Maxwell Bloomfield, *American Lawyers in a Changing Society, 1776–1876* (Cambridge, Mass., 1976), 32–58; Horwitz, *The Transformation of American Law*, 149, 151–52, 154. For important insights into early-nineteenth-century tension between communal norms and the atomistic imperatives of an anticommunal legal

system, see Alfred S. Konefsky and Andrew J. King (eds.), *The Papers of Daniel Webster, Legal Papers: The New Hampshire Practice*, 3 vols. (Hanover, N.H., 1982), I: xxxiii.

4. For the theory and practice of utopian communities, see Rosabeth Moss Kanter, *Commitment and Community* (Cambridge, Mass., 1972), 3–8, 33–49, 76–123; Laurence Veysey, *The Communal Experience* (Chicago, 1973); Arthur E. Bestor, Jr., *Backwoods Utopias* (Philadelphia, 1950).

5. Carol Weisbrod, *The Boundaries of Utopia* (New York, 1980), 9–10. Weisbrod's study is filled with valuable insights, from a legal perspective, into the interplay of legality and informality in utopian communities.

6. Alice Felt Tyler, *Freedom's Ferment* (Minneapolis, 1944), 185–86, 194; John Humphrey Noyes, *History of American Socialisms* (New York, 1870), 295, 619; Spencer C. Olin, Jr., "The Oneida Community and the Instability of Charismatic Authority," 67 *Journal of American History* (September 1980), 285–300; Weisbrod, *The Boundaries of Utopia*, 115–17.

7. *Ibid.*, 116, 117, 118; Frederick Rapp to Samuel Worcester, December 19, 1822, in Karl J. R. Arndt, *Documentary History of the Indiana Decade of the Harmony Society, 1814–1824*, 2 vols. (Indianapolis, 1975), II:512–13.

8. Charles Nordhoff, *The Communistic Societies of the United States* (New York, 1875), 321; William A. Hinds, *American Communities and Cooperative Colonies* (Chicago, 1908), 284, 317, 591; William Hebert, "A Visit to the Colony of Harmony in Indiana," in Harlow Lindley (ed.), *Indiana as Seen by Early Travelers*, 3 *Indiana Historical Collections* (Indianapolis, 1916), 353, 356; Weisbrod, *The Boundaries of Utopia*, 116.

9. Kanter, *Commitment and Community*, 9.

10. Edward D. Andrews, *The People Called Shakers* (New York, 1953), 181, 192; Amelia E. Russell, *Home Life of the Brook Farm Association* (Boston, 1900), 73–75; Marianne Dwight Orvis, *Letters from Brook Farm, 1844–47* (Poughkeepsie, 1928), 62; Tyler, *Freedom's Ferment*, 111, 192–93; Olin, "Oneida Community," 290; [John Humphrey Noyes], *Mutual Criticism* (Syracuse, 1975), xxi–xxv, 29–30, 80; Rapp to Edward P. Page, March 7, 1822, in Arndt, *Documentary History*, II:363–64; Bestor, *Backwoods Utopias*, 172; Noyes, *American Socialisms*, 279, 321, 418; Nordhoff, *Communistic Societies*, 406.

11. Application for Membership, The Kaweah Cooperative Colony, California (1891). I am grateful to Yacov Oved, who shared this item, and his vast knowledge of American and Israeli utopian communities, with me. See Arndt, *Documentary History*, II:187–88, 673; Weisbrod, *The Boundaries of Utopia*, xi–xvi, 14, 34, 62–63, 104–6, 117.

12. *Ibid.*, 14, 117; Olin, "Oneida Community," 287, 293–99; Louis J. Kern, *An Ordered Love* (Chapel Hill, 1981), 53, 295, 298, 313.

13. Olin, "Oneida Community," 299–300.

14. C. Paul Dredge, "Dispute Settlement in the Mormon Community: The Operation of Ecclesiastical Courts in Utah," in Mauro Cappelletti (ed.), *Access to Justice*, 4 vols. (Alphen aan den Rijn and Milan, 1979), IV:199.

15. Mark P. Leone, *Roots of Modern Mormonism* (Cambridge, Mass., 1979), 1–27, 115–18, 120–27, 145–46; Dredge, "Dispute Settlement in the Mormon Community," 193–200, 211.

16. Leone, *Roots of Modern Mormonism*, 26, 114, 116–17; Dredge, "Dispute Settlement in the Mormon Community," 203, 212–14; Orma Linford, "The Mormons, the Law, and the Territory of Utah," 23 *American J. Legal Hist.* (1979), 213–35.

17. Edward Bellamy, *Looking Backward: 2000–1887* (Boston, 1888), 285–86.

18. William S. McFeely, *Yankee Stepfather: General O. O. Howard and the Freedmen* (New Haven, 1968), 149, 156; George R. Bentley, *A History of the Freedmen's Bureau* (Philadelphia, 1955), 149–52.

19. Oliver Otis Howard, *Autobiography*, 2 vols. (New York, 1980), II:252.

20. McFeely, *Yankee Stepfather*, 139–40.

21. *Ibid.*, 73, 154–57, 182.

22. *Report of Brevet Major General O. O. Howard to the Secretary of War* (Washington, D.C., 1869), 14–15; Bentley, *Freedmen's Bureau*, 149–53, 160, 162; Donald G. Nieman, *To Set the Law in Motion: The Freedmen's Bureau and the Legal Rights of Blacks, 1865–1868* (New York, 1979), 8–9, 11, 189, 217.

23. One notable exception, on the Mississippi plantation of Joseph Davis (Jefferson's brother), demonstrated the vitality and longevity of indigenous black dispute settlement. Davis, inspired by the ideals of Robert Owen, founder of the New Harmony utopian community, had established a slave court as part of his commitment to plantation self-government. It retained its independence through the early period of Reconstruction military occupation, deciding freedmen's disputes "according to their Ideas of Justice and the evidence produced." More than a decade later, after the plantation suffered serious financial reverses, Davis Bend blacks retained the Owenite model at their new site of Mound Bayou, where they still excluded formal legal sanctions. See Janet Sharp Hermann, *The Pursuit of a Dream* (New York, 1981), 12–14, 62–63, 101, 221, 227.

24. Joseph D. Weeks, *Labor Differences and Their Settlement: A Plea for Arbitration and Conciliation* (New York, 1886), iii, 12–13, 37, 73–74, 76–77; Edwin E. Witte, *Historical Survey of Labor Arbitration* (Philadelphia, 1952), 1–5; Carroll D. Wright, *Industrial Conciliation and Arbitration* (Boston, 1881), 83–86, 105–7, 161–62, 169–73.

25. Edward Cummings, "Industrial Arbitration in the United States," 9 *Q.J. of Economics* (1895), 3–21.

26. Witte, *Historical Survey*, 7–10; G. C. Clemens, "Industrial Arbitration," 3 *Kans. L.R.* (1886), 113–18; Wright, *Industrial Conciliation*, 85, 133–35; R. W. Fleming, *The Labor Arbitration Process* (Urbana, 1965), 2.

27. John Peter Altgeld, "Arbitration to Prevent Strikes," 19 *Chicago Legal News* (July 30, 1887), 375–77; Conrad Reno, "Arbitration and the Wage Contract," 26 *American L.R.* (1892), 837–39; Civic Federation of Chicago, *Congress on Industrial Conciliation and Arbitration* (Chicago, 1894), 71.

28. *Ibid.*, 20, 35, 37, 41, 47, 59.

29. *Ibid.*, 37, 39–41, 45, 48.

30. Henry Demarest Lloyd, *A Country Without Strikes* (New York, 1900), 13–16, 170–79; Frank Parsons, "Compulsory Arbitration," 17 *Arena* (March 1897), reprinted in Lamar T. Beman (comp.), *Selected Articles on the Compulsory Arbitration and Compulsory Investigation of Industrial Disputes* (New York, 1920), 97–8, 101.

31. National Civic Federation, *Industrial Conciliation* (New York, 1902), 4–5, 92–98, 211.

32. *Ibid.*, 213; Frank T. Carlton, "The Advantages and Defects of Compulsory Arbitration," 69 *Annals of American Academy of Political and Social Science* (January 1917), 153, 156; John A. Fitch, "Industrial Peace by Law—The Kansas Way," 44 *Survey* (April 3, 1920), 7–8, 48; Beman, *Selected Articles*, 156.

33. For an excellent analysis of the destructive impact of industrialization in one community, and the futile efforts to restore it with arbitration, see Alan Dawley, *Class and Community: The Industrial Revolution in Lynn* (Cambridge, Mass., 1976), 174–88.

34. Robert L. Hale, "Law Making by Unofficial Minorities," 20 *Columbia L.R.* (1920), 451–56; O. William Ross, "Historical Background and Perspective," in Maurice S. Trotta, *Labor Arbitration* (New York, 1961), 13–15; Julius G. Getman, "Labor Arbitration and Dispute Resolution," 88 *Yale L.J.* (1979), 916–17; Frances Kellor, *American Arbitration: Its History, Functions and Achievements* (New York, 1948), 6–7. Once the labor movement secured its New Deal gains, labor arbitration became an adjunct of labor law. With its legalization came encouragement of precedent, formal briefs and opinions, and the extensive participation of lawyers as arbitrators. At "every stage of the process," according to Getman, "there are factors enhancing the value of formality and legalism." Getman, "Labor Arbitration," 920–21.

35. Jonathan Garlock, "The Knights of Labor Courts: A Case Study of Popular Justice," in Richard L. Abel (ed.), *The Politics of Informal Justice*, vol. I, *The American Experience* (New York, 1982), 27–31; Clyde W. Summers, "The Law of Union Discipline: What the Courts Do in Fact," 70 *Yale L.J.* (1960), 178–79, 184, 198–206.

III. LAW AND ACCULTURATION: IMMIGRANT EXPERIENCES

1. For a suggestive hypothesis about internal fragmentation among immigrant groups, who seemed united only to outsiders, see Jonathan D. Sarna, "From Immigrants to Ethnics: Toward a New Theory of 'Ethnicization,'" 5 *Ethnicity* (1978), 370–78.

2. Alexander De Conde, *Half Bitter, Half Sweet* (New York, 1971), 86–87; Theodore Saloutos, *The Greeks in the United States* (Cambridge, Mass., 1964), 48.

3. Saloutos, *The Greeks*, 76–77, 133, 285.

4. In addition to the books cited above, there are valuable insights into the acculturation process among southern and eastern European immigrants in Josef J. Barton, *Peasants and Strangers* (Cambridge, Mass., 1975); Victor Greene, *For God and Country* (Madison, 1975).

5. Nicolay Grevstad, "Norway's Conciliation Tribunals," 2 *J. Am. Jud. S.* (June 1918), 5–7. Conciliation and mediation are similar forms of third-party intervention, agreed to by disputants. They are distinguished from arbitration, in which the disputants consent to be bound by a third party, and adjudication, which involves third-party intervention and a binding decision by a government tribunal, whether or not the parties are willing. Historically, however, these distinctions were less clear.

6. Herbert Harley, "Justice or Litigation," 6 *Va. L.R.* (1919), 150; "North Dakota Legislature Enacts Law for Conciliation Procedure," 4 *J. Am. Jud. Soc.* (April 1921), 165–66; "Conciliation Law Held Valid," 6 *J. Am. Jud. Soc.* (February 1923), 133–53; "Minneapolis Conciliation Court," 2 *J. Am. Jud. Soc.* (June 1918), 16; "Conciliation Courts and Procedure Provided for Minnesota Cities," 5 *J. Am. Jud. Soc.* (June 1921), 25; William R. Vance, "A Proposed Court of Conciliation," 1 *Minn. L.R.* (1917), 110–11, 114–16. The North Dakota conciliation statute was challenged on the ground that it was an unconstitutional denial of the right to a jury trial. *Klein v. Hutton*, 191 N.W. (1922), 485.

7. Jerome Alan Cohen, "Chinese Mediation on the Eve of Modernization," 54 *Calif. L.R.* (1966), 1201, 1205–7; Stanley Lubman, "Mao and Mediation: Politics and Dispute Resolution in Communist China," 55 *Calif. L.R.* (1967), 1286–91.

8. Cohen, "Chinese Mediation," 1203, 1207, 1214–15, 1224.

9. Leigh-Wai Doo, "Dispute Settlement in Chinese-American Communities," 21 *American J. of Comparative Law* (1973), 629–33, 636; Gunther Barth, *Bitter Strength: A History of the Chinese in the United States 1850–1870* (Cambridge, Mass., 1964); Chu Chai, "Administration of Law Among the Chinese in Chicago," 22 *J. Criminal Law and Criminology* (1932), 806–8; *People v. Hall*, 4 *California Reports* (1854), 405.

10. Stanford M. Lyman, "Contrasts in the Community Organization of

Chinese and Japanese in North America," 5 *Canadian R. of Sociology and Anthropology* (1968), 52–54, 64; Lyman, "Conflict and the Web of Group Affiliation in San Francisco's Chinatown, 1850–1910," in Norris Hundley, Jr. (ed.), *The Asian-American: The Historical Experience* (Santa Barbara, 1976), 27–28, 48, 52.

11. *Ibid.*, 29, 37; Chai, "Administration of Law," 812, 816; Victor G. Nee and Brett de Bary Nee, *Longtime Californ'* (New York, 1972), 63–67, 229; Barth, *Bitter Strength*, 84; Remigio B. Ronquillo, "The Administration of Law Among the Chinese in Chicago," 25 *J. of Criminal Law and Criminology* (1934), 211, 221–23. A prefatory note to Ronquillo's article indicates that after the Chai study had been published two years earlier, Chinese leaders in Chicago refused to permit further study of their dispute-settlement institutions. According to Chai, there were no complete written case reports to study.

12. Barth, *Bitter Strength*, 80–81, 84–86, 92–93, 167; Nee and Nee, *Longtime Californ'*, 64–67.

13. Doo, "Dispute Settlement in Chinese-American Communities," 638, 644–45, 651–55; Rose Hum Lee, "The Decline of Chinatowns in the United States," 54 *Amer. J. of Sociology* (1949), 422–32; Roger Grace, "Justice, Chinese Style," 75 *Case & Comment* (January–February 1970), 50–51; Nee and Nee, *Longtime Californ'*, 184–87. For a similar historical and cultural pattern in Japan, see Takeyoshi Kawashima, "Dispute Resolution in Japan," in Vilhelm Aubert (ed.), *Sociology of Law* (Baltimore, 1969), 182–92. The extent of Oriental acculturation within the American legal system can be measured symbolically by a recent report that when the Ninth Circuit Court of Appeals convened in San Francisco, the three-judge panel consisted of a Korean-American, a Japanese-American, and a Chinese-American. "Land of Immigrants," *New York Times* (November 11, 1980). But for the persistence of traditional patterns of disputing in Chinatown to this day, see Sally Engle Merry, "Going to Court: Strategies of Dispute Management in an American Urban Neighborhood," 13 *Law and Society R.* (1979), 913–16.

14. See Harold J. Berman, *The Interaction of Law and Religion* (Nashville, 1974), 24; Milton R. Konvitz, *Judaism and the American Idea* (Ithaca, 1978), 53–54, 104–5; Salo W. Baron, *The Jewish Community*, 3 vols. (Philadelphia, 1942), II:208–9; Leo Landman, *Jewish Law in the Diaspora: Confrontation and Accommodation* (Philadelphia, 1968), 15–23, 58, 62–67, 88–89; Aaron M. Schreiber, *Jewish Law and Decision-Making* (Philadelphia, 1979), 242; *Pentateuch with Rashi's Commentary*, trans. M. Rosenbaum and A. M. Silberman (New York, n.d.), "Exodus," 108 n; David M. Shohet, *The Jewish Court in the Middle Ages* (New York, 1931), 95–97, 105; Solomon Ganzfried, *Code of Jewish Law* (New York, 1961), 67; *Reflections of the Rav*, Lessons in Jewish Thought Adopted from the Lectures

of Rabbi Joseph B. Soloveitchick by Rabbi Abraham R. Besdin (Jerusalem, 1979), 53–58.

15. Shohet, *The Jewish Court*, 159, 198, 200–203; Baron, *Jewish Community*, 236–45; Schreiber, *Jewish Law*, 391–92.

16. Landman, *Jewish Law*, 90, 101, 103, 135–38.

17. See, for example, Selig Adler and Thomas E. Connolly, *From Ararat to Suburbia* (Philadelphia, 1960), 160–213, 250.

18. Moses Rischin, *The Promised City: New York's Jews, 1870–1914* (Cambridge, Mass., 1962), 147; Arthur A. Goren, *New York Jews and the Quest for Community* (New York, 1970), 42–56, 82–83.

19. Goren, *New York Jews*, 196–211.

20. B. H. Hartogensis, "A Successful Community Court," 12 *J. Amer. Jud. Soc.* (April 1929), 182. For Magnes's lobbying efforts, see Magnes to Sen. Robert F. Wagner and Assemblyman Alfred E. Smith, February 12, 1915, File 1848, Judah L. Magnes MSS, Central Archives for the History of the Jewish People, Jerusalem. An unidentified *Kehillah* document (File 1853/23–4) relates such efforts to the Municipal Court Act of 1915, which removed impediments to small-claims arbitration.

21. For responses to the Baltimore arbitration experiment, and the emphasis on harmony, see Magnes to S. M. Stroock, April 5, 1914, File 1848; William Liebermann, "Address and Report in Relation to the Establishment of a Court of Arbitration by the Kehillah of the City of New York" (April 1914), File 1848; "Report Upon Proposed Court of Arbitration," File 1854; William Liebermann to H. P. Mendes, April 4, 1919, File 1850; Liebermann to Meyer Linchner, April 16, 1920, File 1853; Liebermann to William Jacobson, April 26, 1920, File 1853, Magnes MSS; Goren, *New York Jews*, 198–99.

22. *Kehillah* documents, File 1853/23–4; "Kehillah Arbitration Courts" (n.d.), File 1854, Magnes MSS.

23. Goren, *New York Jews*, 3–17, 247–52, offers a perceptive analysis; the quotations appear on pp. 3, 252. See Rabbi S. L. Hurwitz, "Jewish Ministers' Association of America," in *The Jewish Communal Register of New York City, 1917–1918* (New York, 1918), 1189–90. Professor Goren called this item to my attention and helped me locate the Arbitration Court in its Jewish cultural context.

24. Samuel Buchler, *"Cohen Comes First" and Other Cases: Stories of Controversies Before the New York Jewish Court of Arbitration* (New York, 1933), vii–xv; James Yaffe, *So Sue Me! The Story of a Community Court* (New York, 1972), 7–8; Israel Goldstein, *Toward a Solution* (New York, 1940), 305–6; Goldstein, *Jewish Justice and Conciliation* (New York, 1981), xxviii, 102–3.

25. Buchler, *"Cohen Comes First,"* xiii, 205ff; Goldstein, *Toward A Solution*, 319–20; Yaffe, *So Sue Me!*, 9–12, 15–24, 53–62, 265–69. In addition

to the disputes recounted in these volumes, and in Goldstein, *Jewish Justice*, the case records of the Jewish Conciliation Court comprise a large segment of the Israel Goldstein MSS, Central Zionist Archives, Jerusalem.

26. Louis Richman to Israel Goldstein, January 10, 1929; Jewish Conciliation Court, Certificate of Incorporation, December 5, 1930; Israel Goldstein Address, January 27, 1932, File 271a, Israel Goldstein MSS; interview with Israel Goldstein, July 1, 1981.

27. E.g., Goldstein to Edward L. Wertheim, February 15, 1930; Goldstein to Irving Lehman, October 16, 1931, File 274; Goldstein to Altman Foundation, June 15, 1931; Goldstein to David Brown, March 24, 1932; Goldstein to Simon Bergman, January 19, 1934, File 273, Goldstein MSS.

28. Goldstein, *Jewish Justice*, 212; Goldstein to Irving Lehman, October 16, 1931, File 274; Contribution Request, February 9, 1931; Richman to Goldstein, June 12, 1931; Goldstein Address, January 27, 1932, File 271a, Goldstein MSS; Buchler, *"Cohen Comes First,"* 205.

29. Goldstein Address, January 27, 1932, File 271a; Goldstein to Richman, August 23, 1934, File 271b; Minutes of Annual Meeting, January 12, 1938, Goldstein MSS. There are many letters in the Goldstein Papers that illuminate Rabbi Goldstein's preoccupation with Buchler's court. Unfortunately, these are now inaccessible to scholars. In the author's presence, Rabbi Goldstein, claiming to protect Jewish honor, removed perhaps two dozen letters pertaining to the Buchler court from his files. Subsequently, he refused to permit me to use nine additional letters, on the same subject, which he previously had allowed me to examine. Old issues die hard, as suggested by Goldstein's reference to that conflict as "the original sin." The real issue, however, has less to do with honor or sin than with the assimilationist impulses and class elitism of the Goldstein court.

30. Goldstein Press Statement, December 2, 1936, File 271c; Jewish Conciliation Court Press Release, January 13, 1937; Minutes of Annual Meeting, January 12, 1938; Goldstein to Richman, April 9, 1939, File 271e; Richman to Goldstein, February 1, 1949, File 274, Goldstein MSS; Goldstein, *Jewish Justice*, Appendix III, 220–35. New York courts, for different reasons that touched similar issues of power and control, were also critical of "swing-time justice." See Richman to Goldstein, April 22, 1940, File 271e, Goldstein MSS.

31. Goldstein to Richman, November 30, 1931, File 271a; Richman to Goldstein, December 8, 1939, File 271e; Richman to Goldstein, April 24, May 6, October 22, 1941, File 271f, Goldstein MSS. Even so, the court was criticized for its own breaches of decorum. See Annual Report of the Executive Secretary (1931), File 271a; Memo of Conference between Richman and Frances Taussig, January 8, 1935, File 271c; Richman to Goldstein, April 24, 1941, File 271f; David Brown to Goldstein, April 30, 1931, File 273, Goldstein MSS.

32. Address of Israel Goldstein, January 27, 1932, File 271a; Goldstein to Simon Bergman, January 19, 1934, File 273, Goldstein MSS.

33. Report of the Executive Secretary (1932), File 271a; David Brown to Goldstein, April 30, 1931, File 273; Goldstein to Richman, January 13, 1941; Richman to Goldstein, January 15, 1941, File 271f; Richman to Goldstein, September 14, 1932; Goldstein to Richman, December 10, 1934, File 271a; Richman to Jacob R. Schiff, December 12, 1933, File 274; Goldstein to Richman, January 12, 1942, File 271f, Goldstein MSS. For the photograph, see Goldstein, *Jewish Justice*, following p. 92.

34. Richman to Goldstein, February 2, 1937; Goldstein to Richman, February 11, 1937, File 271d; Richman to Goldstein, April 12, 1939, File 271e; Max Steuer to Schiff, June 6, 1939; Richman to Steuer, June 7, 1939, File 274, Goldstein MSS.

35. "Rabbinical Courts: Modern Day Solomons," 6 *Columbia J. of Law and Social Action* (1970), 61, 69–70, 75; Harvey J. Kirsch, "Conflict Resolution and the Legal Culture: A Study of the Rabbinical Court," 9 *Osgoode Hall L.J.* (1971), 339–40, 347–48, 353–56. See also Frank Fishkin, "The Bet Din as an Arbitration Model," 84 *Case and Comment* (November–December 1979), 50–54.

36. For a detailed account, see Jerold S. Auerbach, "From Rags to Robes: The Legal Profession, Social Mobility and the American Jewish Experience," 66 *Amer. Jewish Hist. Q.* (December 1976), 249–84.

37. See H. N. Hirsch, *The Enigma of Felix Frankfurter* (New York, 1981), 23, 148, 173.

38. The best analysis of Bickel's thought appears in Edward A. Purcell, Jr., "Alexander M. Bickel and the Post-Realist Constitution," 11 *Harvard Civil Rights–Civil Liberties L.R.* (1976), 548, 553–54, 559–60. See Shlomo Bickel, "Three Generations—A Memoir." 34 *Commentary* (October 1962), 324–33; Alexander M. Bickel, *The Morality of Consent* (New Haven, 1975), 120–23; Alfred S. Konefsky, "Men of Great and Little Faith: Generations of Constitutional Scholars," 30 *Buffalo L.R.* (1981), 375–81.

39. Abe Fortas, "Thurman Arnold and the Theater of the Law," 79 *Yale L.J.* (1970), 998. For an illuminating exploration of the Jewish infighting between the Hoffmans, see John Murray Cuddihy, *The Ordeal of Civility* (New York, 1974), 191–95; for examples, see Mark L. Levine, George C. McNamee, Daniel Greenberg (eds.), *The Tales of Hoffman* (New York, 1970), 188, 232–34.

40. Evelyn Balderman, "Jewish Courts" (unpublished ms., 1974), 44; Solomon Poll, *The Hasidic Community of Williamsburg* (New York, 1962), 71; Murray Schumach, "The City's Most Exclusive Club," *New York Times Magazine* (May 6, 1979), 108–13; Schumach, *The Diamond People* (New York, 1981), 38–41; Isaac Bashevis Singer, *In My Father's Court* (New York, 1965), viii.

41. For an instructive example of the cultural conflicts that resulted from the imposition of Anglo-Saxon legal procedure in a colonial setting, with themes appropriate to the immigrant experience in the United States, see Bernard S. Cohn, "Some Notes on Law and Change in North India," in Paul Bohannan (ed.), *Law and Warfare* (Austin, Texas, 1967), 155–59.

IV. THE COMMERCIALIZATION OF COMMUNITY

1. Roscoe Pound, "Social Justice and Legal Justice," 30 Mo. Bar Ass'n *Proc.* (1912), 110, 112; Reginald Heber Smith, *Justice and the Poor* (New York, 1919), 15.

2. For the best contemporary explication of these developments, and the relation between them, see Smith, *Justice and the Poor*, chs. 3–7, pp. 83–84.

3. Roscoe Pound, "The Limits of Effective Legal Action," 3 *American Bar Ass'n J.* (January 1917), 55–57; Pound, *An Introduction to the Philosophy of Law* (New Haven, 1922), 54.

4. Barbara Yngvesson and Patricia Hennessey, "Small Claims, Complex Disputes: A Review of the Small Claims Literature," 9 *Law & Society R.* (1974–75), 221–22; Reginald Heber Smith, "The Danish Conciliation System," 11 *J. Am. Jud. Soc.* (October 1927), 86.

5. Manuel Levine, "The Conciliation Court of Cleveland," American Judicature Society, Bulletin VIII, *Informal Procedure* (1915), 4–6, 11–12, 16–17 (according to Levine's figures, 7,000 cases before the Municipal Court were resolved by conciliation from 1913 to 1918); Smith, *Justice and the Poor*, 60–61, 63. The Cleveland conciliation experiment received favorable notice on the grounds of speed, simplicity, equality, and cheapness in the provision of justice for poor people. E.g., John H. Wigmore, Introduction to *Informal Procedure*, 23; Smith, *Justice and the Poor*, 66.

6. "Informal Procedure in Chicago," 2 *J. Am. Jud. Soc.* (August 1918), 26; William F. Willoughby, *Principles of Judicial Administration* (Washington, D.C., 1929), 314; 39 New York State Bar Assoc. *Reports* (1916), 295–96; Smith, *Justice and the Poor*, 63–64; "Try Conciliation in Iowa," 7 *J. Am. Jud. Soc.* (June 1923), 15.

7. Edgar J. Lauer, "Conciliation and Arbitration in the Municipal Court of the City of New York," 1 *J. Am. Jud. Soc.* (February 1918), 155; F. R. Aumann, "The Des Moines Conciliation Court," 12 *J. Am. Jud. Soc.* (June 1928), 22–23; Reginald Heber Smith, "The Place of Conciliation in the Administration of Justice," 9 *American Bar Ass'n J.* (November 1923), 746–47; Willoughby, *Principles*, 42; Smith, *Justice and the Poor*, 51.

8. "Conference of Bar Association Delegates," 9 *American Bar Ass'n J.* (November 1923), 749–51.

9. Reginald Heber Smith, "The Elimination of Delay Through Small

Claims Courts and Conciliation Tribunals," 10 Academy of Political Science *Proc.* (1923), 529.

10. *Ibid.*, 530; Reginald Heber Smith, "Small Claims Courts for Massachusetts," 4 *J. Am. Jud. Soc.* (August 1920), 51–53; Smith, "Conciliation and Legal Aid: An Opportunity for Pioneering," 136 *Annals* (March 1928), 61–63; Smith, *Justice and the Poor,* 60; Herbert Harley, "Conciliation Is Succeeding," 4 *J. Am. Jud. Soc.* (October 1920), 74, 76; Harley, "Conciliation Procedure in Small Cases," 124 *Annals* (March 1926), 91–97.

11. "Report of Committee on Small Claims and Conciliation Procedure," Conference of Bar Association Delegates, 10 *American Bar Ass'n J.* (November 1924), 820–30; 39 New York State Bar Association *Reports* (1916), 298; "Informal Procedure in Chicago," 2 *J. Am. Jud. Soc.* (June 1918), 24–25.

12. Smith, *Justice and the Poor,* 13; Pound, "Limits of Effective Legal Action," 65–70; Smith, "Elimination of Delay," 522; Yngvesson and Hennessey, "Small Claims Courts," 228ff. A more favorable assessment appears in John C. Ruhnka and Steven Weller, *Small Claims Courts* (Williamsburg, Va., 1978).

13. Smith, "Elimination of Delay," 527.

14. Ellis W. Hawley, *The New Deal and the Problem of Monopoly* (Princeton, 1966), 10–11, 35; "Let's Arbitrate It," 132 *Printer's Ink* (August 20, 1925), 101–4.

15. Clarence F. Birdseye, *Arbitration and Business Ethics* (New York, 1926), 87–89; Elliott F. Shepard, "The Court of Arbitration: Its Advantages and Importance to Business Men," Address to Chamber of Commerce (October 7, 1875) with Remarks of E. L. Fancher, American Arbitration Association Archives, New York City; American Arbitration Association, *Decennial Report, 1926–1936*; William Catron Jones, "Three Centuries of Commercial Arbitration in New York: A Brief Survey," 5 *Wash. U. Law Q.* (1956), 216–17; Charles T. Gwynne, "The Oldest American Tribunal," 1 *Arb. J.* (April 1937), 118–19.

16. Birdseye, *Arbitration and Business Ethics,* 5–6, 36, 44–46; Franklin D. Jones, *Trade Association Activities and the Law* (New York, 1922), 194–201; "Commercial Arbitration Developed in Trade Courts," 7 *J. Am. Jud. Soc.* (June 1923), 10–13. For a comprehensive listing of the dates when arbitration was established in various industries and exchanges, see American Arbitration Association, *Yearbook on Commercial Arbitration* (New York, 1927).

17. Birdseye, *Arbitration and Business Ethics,* 94–96, 98–99; Committee on Arbitration, Chamber of Commerce, to NYSBA, October 6, 1915, 39 NYSBA *Reports* (1916), 263.

18. Jonathan Lurie, "Private Associations, Internal Regulation and Progressivism: The Chicago Board of Trade, 1880–1923, as a Case Study," 16 *American J. Legal Hist.* (1972), 221, 236–37. Lurie's analysis suggests that

the commodities exchanges and the major boards of trade consistently opposed federal regulation of their activities, 1890–1916. This set them apart from those industries seeking regulation for their own protection, the thesis of Gabriel R. Kolko, *The Triumph of Conservatism* (New York, 1963). See also "Promoting Commercial Arbitration," 2 *J. Am. Jud. Soc.* (April 1919), 185; "Commercial Arbitration Developed in Trade Courts," 7 *J. Am. Jud. Soc.* (June 1923), 7–14.

19. Willoughby, *Principles of Judicial Administration*, 7–26; Francis R. Aumann, *The Changing American Legal System* (Columbus, 1940), 226–34; Percy Werner, "Voluntary Tribunals," 32 Mo. Bar Ass'n *Proc.* (1914), 146.

20. *Ibid.*, 154–58.

21. Werner, "Voluntary Tribunals," 3 *J. Am. Jud. Soc.* (December 1919), 102; 38 NYSBA *Reports* (1915), 378–403, 412–14; 39 (1916), 255–57; 40 (1917), 366–67, 398–99, 404.

22. Julius Henry Cohen, *Commercial Arbitration and the Law* (New York, 1918), *passim*; Chamber of Commerce, "A Brief History of Commercial Arbitration in New York" (New York, 1922); 42 NYSBA *Reports* (1919), 92–93, and 43 (1920), 97; Frances Kellor, *Arbitration and the Legal Profession* (New York, 1952), 41, 46.

23. Julius Henry Cohen, "Commercial Arbitration—Its Scope and Limitations," address delivered May 17, 1923, 4–8, 11–12; Cohen, "Commercial Arbitration and the New York Statute," 31 *Yale L.J.* (1921), 147–60. For an analysis of Cohen's preference for contract over regulation, see Gerald Fetner, "Public Power and Professional Responsibility: Julius Henry Cohen and the Origins of the Public Authority," 21 *American J. Legal Hist.* (October 1977), 21, 23.

24. Report of the Conference of Bar Association Delegates, 5 *American Bar Ass'n J.* (January 1919), 54–60; 50 ABA *Reports* (1925), 152–56.

25. Report of the Conference of Bar Association Delegates, 45–51.

26. Arbitration Society of America, Letter of Invitation, June 14, 1922; Minutes, Meeting at Lawyers Club, June 20, 1922, AAA Archives.

27. Minutes, Meeting at Residence of Mrs. Vincent Astor, February 28, 1923, AAA Archives; B. J. Duncan, "Business Turns Its Back on Litigation," 16 *Forbes* (May 1, 1925), 96; Moses H. Grossman, "The Need of Arbitration to Relieve the Congestion in the Courts," 10 Academy of Political Science *Proc.* (July 1923), 518–20; Address by Moses H. Grossman, January 13, 1928, copy in AAA Archives.

28. Arbitration Society of America, "The Project in Outline"; newspaper editorials (1922) from *NY Commercial Evening Mail, Evening World*, and unidentified sources, AAA Archives; 1 *Arb. News* (January 1924).

29. Minutes of Meeting, February 28, 1923, AAA Archives.

30. Kellor, *Arbitration and the Legal Profession*, 43–44; Grossman, "The Need of Arbitration," 517; Certification of Incorporation of Arbitration

Foundation (January 23, 1925); Kenneth Dayton to Kellor, June 23, 1925; Agreement between Arbitration Society of America and Arbitration Foundation, January 29, 1926, AAA Archives; Kellor, *American Arbitration: Its History, Functions, and Achievements* (New York, 1948), 13–18.

31. Martin Domke, *Commercial Arbitration* (Englewood Cliffs, N.J., 1965), 2; Moses H. Grossman notes, Address to AAA Membership Campaign Luncheon, March 9, 1927, AAA Archives; Carl F. Taeusch, "Extrajudicial Settlement of Controversies," 83 *U. Pa. L.R.* (1934), 147–51; "Advantages Ascribed to Arbitration," 9 *J. Am. Jud. Soc.* (October 1925), 75–76; "Where Jury Trial Fails," 9 *J. Am. Jud. Soc.* (October 1925), 71–73; *Yearbook on Commercial Arbitration in the United States* (New York, 1927), vii–viii; Chamber of Commerce of the State of New York, Committee on Arbitration, *Report* (1916); Charles L. Bernheimer, "The Advantages of Arbitration Procedure," 124 *Annals* (March 1926), 98; AAA, *Suggestions for the Practice of Commercial Arbitration in the United States* (New York, 1928), 4; Harris J. Griston, "The Substitution of Arbitration for Litigation," 2 *NYU L.R.* (1925), 111; Wesley A. Sturges, "Commercial Arbitration of Court Application of the Common Law Rules of Marketing," 9 *J. Am. Jud. Soc.* (October 1925), 90n. See also Stewart Macaulay, "Non-Contractual Relations in Business: A Preliminary Study," 28 *Am. Soc. R.* (1963), 60–61, 65.

32. Wesley A. Sturges, *A Treatise on Commercial Arbitrations and Awards* (Kansas City, 1930), iii; Paul L. Sayre, "Development of Commercial Arbitration Law," 37 *Yale L.J.* (1928), 613; Carl E. Herring, "The Lawyer's Relation to Arbitration," 12 *J. Am. Jud. Soc.* (February 1929), 155; Frances Kellor, *Arbitration in the New Industrial Society* (New York, 1934), 19.

33. *Ibid.*, 279–80; New York Chamber of Commerce, Committee on Arbitration, *Report* (1921), 5; James B. Boskey, "A History of Commercial Arbitration in New Jersey," 18 *Rutgers-Camden L.J.* (1977), 285.

34. Philip G. Phillips, "Arbitration and Conflicts of Laws: A Study of Benevolent Compulsion," 19 *Cornell L.Q.* (1934), 198; Joseph Wheless, "Arbitration as a Judicial Process of Law," 30 *W. Va. L.Q.* (1924), 218; Kellor, *Arbitration in the New Industrial Society*, 19; Sayre, "Development of Commercial Arbitration Law," 614–15; Osmond K. Fraenkel, "The New York Arbitration Law," 32 *Columbia L.R.* (1932), 638–41; "Arbitration and Award: Commercial Arbitration in California," 17 *Cal. L.R.* (1929), 646; Clifton F. Weidlich, "A Test of Compulsory Arbitration in New York," 4 *Conn. Bar J.* (April 1930), 95–98, 103; J. Noble Braden, "Sound Rules and Administration in Arbitration," 83 *U. Pa. L.R.* (1934), 189–91. Wheless, a lawyer-member of the Arbitration Society of America, commended arbitration for its "prompt and economical rendering to every man his just due *in law*," 211 (italics added). Fraenkel presented citations to more than one

hundred cases in just fifteen pages of text, which suggests the range and frequency of arbitration litigation. For reference to a 1934 arbitration proceeding involving 162 hearings, 8,000 pages of testimony, $450,000 in expenses, and no decision, see Heinrich Kronstein, "Business Arbitration— Instrument of Private Government," 54 *Yale L.J.* (1944), 39n.

35. Carl F. Taeusch, *Policy and Ethics in Business* (New York, 1931), 590; Soia Mentschikoff, "Commercial Arbitration," 61 *Columbia L.R.* (1961), 856–58. Overheard in the AAA Library (in 1979), from one archivist to another in response to a telephone inquiry: "I think he should speak to someone in our legal department."

36. Kellor, *Arbitration and the Legal Profession*, 48–49; Domke, *Commercial Arbitration*, 14; Mentschikoff, "Commercial Arbitration," 858–61; Kellor, *American Arbitration*, 24–26; Nathan Isaacs review, 40 *Yale L.J.* (1930), 150; Steven Lazarus et al., *Resolving Business Disputes* (New York, 1965), 66. For figures showing the steady rise of arbitration by the mid-1920s, see AAA, *Yearbook on Commercial Arbitration* (1927), 614; AAA, *Third Annual Report of the President* (1929), 26; AAA, *Decennial Report* (1936), 8.

37. Nathan Isaacs, review of Sturges, *Treatise*, 40 *Yale L.J.* (1930), 149–51. Isaacs also suggested how courts had already limited the subjects of arbitration (excluding real estate, probate, and divorce), scrutinized arbitration agreements with especial care, and made submission to arbitration "a precariously technical matter" (149).

38. Isaacs review, 40 *Yale L.J.*, 149–51. For an earlier, less critical analysis, cf. his "Two Views of Commercial Arbitration," 40 *Harvard L.R.* (1927), 929–42; Phillips, "The Paradox in Arbitration Law: Compulsion as Applied to a Voluntary Proceeding," 46 *Harvard L.R.* (1933), 1258–80.

39. Phillips was a Harvard Law School graduate (Class of 1927) who left private practice in Boston in 1934 to work for the National Labor Relations Board. His support of arbitration can be found in "The Paradox in Arbitration Law," 1279; his major critical articles included "Commercial Arbitration under the N.R.A.," 1 *U. Chicago L.R.* (1933–34), 424–40; "Rules of Law or Laissez-Faire in Commercial Arbitration," 47 *Harvard L.R.* (1934), 590–627; "A Lawyer's Approach to Commercial Arbitration," 44 *Yale L.J.* (1934), 31–52.

40. Phillips, "A General Introduction," 83 *U. Pa. L.R.* (1934), 119–21, 125; Phillips, "Commercial Arbitration Under the N.R.A.," 429, 432; Phillips, "A Lawyer's Approach," 43.

41. AAA, *Yearbook on Commercial Arbitration* (1927), 533 (other examples can be found in Phillips, "Rules of Law," 609n, 626n); Phillips, "Rules of Law," 591, 597, 601, 609, 616–17; Phillips, "Commercial Arbitration Under the N.R.A.," 432–44. See the Symposium in 83 *U. Pa. L.R.* (1934), 119–245.

42. A similar reassessment of legal realism is analyzed in Edward A. Purcell, Jr., *The Crisis of Democratic Theory* (Lexington, Ky., 1963), ch. 9; Kronstein, "Business Arbitration," 36, 40–44, 60–61, 66–68. Kronstein was a special attorney in the Department of Justice and a professor of law at Georgetown University.

43. Soia Mentschikoff, "The Significance of Arbitration—A Preliminary Inquiry," 17 *Law and Contemporary Problems* (1952), 699; Kenneth S. Carlston, "Theory of the Arbitration Process," 17 *Law and Contemporary Problems* (1952), 631–32, 635, 651; Kronstein, "Arbitration Is Power," 38 *NYU L.R.* (1963), 662–64, 667–700. For the 1920s see 50 ABA *Reports* (1925), 137, 152–56.

44. Wesley A. Sturges, "Reduction of Costs by Arbitration Procedure," 84 *Paper Trade J.* (June 9, 1927), 49; "Arbitration *versus* Litigation," 7 *Public Utilities Fortnightly* (May 14, 1931), 615. Taeusch suggested that the willingness of lawyers to permit diversion from the legal system indicates only that the disputes are "trivial or inconsequential or relatively too complex for the fee involved." "Extrajudicial Settlement," 152–53.

V. THE LEGALIZATION OF COMMUNITY

1. Edgar S. and Jean C. Cahn, "What Price Justice: The Civilian Perspective Revisited," 41 *Notre Dame Lawyer* (1966), 921–60. For relevant historical background, see Jerold S. Auerbach, *Unequal Justice* (New York, 1976), 263–70.

2. Paul Wahrhaftig, "Citizen Dispute Resolution: A Blue Chip Investment in Community Growth," *Pretrial Services Annual J.* (1978), 2–13; Wahrhaftig, "An Overview of Community-Oriented Citizen Dispute Resolution Programs in the United States," in Richard L. Abel (ed.), *The Politics of Informal Justice*, vol. I, The American Experience (New York, 1982), 75–76; Nils Christie, "Conflicts as Property," 17 *British J. of Criminology* (1977), 1–8; William L. F. Felstiner, Richard L. Abel, and Austin Sarat, "The Emergence and Transformation of Disputes: Naming, Blaming, Claiming . . . ," Working Paper 1981-1, Disputes Processing Research Program (Madison, 1981), 22.

3. Jerome T. Barrett, "Mediation: An Alternative to Violence," 47 *J. Urban Law* (1969), 157–63, and Arnold Zack, "Mediation, Arbitration and the Poverty Program," 2 *Law in Action* (1968), 17, 20–21, are representative examples. For a debate over the efficacy of the labor-relations analogy, see Alfred W. Blumrosen, "Civil Rights Conflicts: The Uneasy Search for Peace in Our Time," 27 *Arb. J.* (1972), 35–46; George Nicolau and Gerald W. Cormick, "Community Disputes and the Resolution of Conflict: Another View," 27 *Arb. J.* (1972), 98-112. The correct analogy, suggested by Professor Marc Feldman, is that 1930s labor mediation and 1960s alternative

dispute settlement both constituted attempts to undercut potentially radical political movements by confining them to institutionalized procedures. For application of the analogy to campus protest, see Sam Zagoria, "Mediation: A Path to Campus Peace?" 92 *Monthly Labor R.* (1969), 9. The Institute for Mediation and Conflict Resolution was established in New York in 1970 to test whether labor-management conflict-resolution techniques might be applied in urban neighborhoods. James H. Laue, "Urban Conflict—What Role for Negotiations and Mediation?" Institute for Mediation and Conflict Resolution (New York, 1971), 1–5.

4. James L. Gibbs, Jr., "The Kpelle Moot," in Paul Bohannan (ed.), *Law and Warfare* (New York, 1967), 277–89; Richard Danzig, "Toward the Creation of a Complementary, Decentralized System of Criminal Justice," 26 *Stanford L.R.* (1973), 3n, 41–48.

5. *Ibid.*, 46–48. For a critique, and Danzig's reply, see William L. F. Felstiner, "Influences of Social Organization on Dispute Processing," 9 *Law & Society R.* (1974), 63–89; Richard Danzig and Michael J. Lowy, "Everyday Disputes and Mediation in the United States: A Reply to Professor Felstiner," 9 *Law & Society R.* (1975), 675–94.

6. Laura Nader and Harry F. Todd, Jr., "Introduction," in Nader and Todd (eds.), *The Disputing Process—Law in Ten Societies* (New York, 1978), 16–38; Carol Greenhouse, "Alternatives to Litigation: An Anthropological View," 2 *New Directions in Legal Services* (1977), 84–85; Donald J. Black, "The Mobilization of Law," 2 *J. Legal Studies* (1973), 134; Austin Sarat and Joel B. Grossman, "Courts and Conflict Resolution: Problems in the Mobilization of Adjudication," 69 *American Political Science R.* (1975), 1209. For an optimistic assessment of transplantation possibilities, see Cathie J. Witty, *Mediation and Society: Conflict Management in Lebanon* (New York, 1980), 90–93, 112–13, 125–26. I am more persuaded by the contrary evidence in Nader and Todd, and in Sally Engle Merry, "Cows or Counselors: Mediation in Village and Pastoral Societies with Implications for American Experiments in Informal Justice" (unpublished ms., 1979), 2, 31–39; Sally Engle Merry and Susan Silbey, "Can Community Dispute Settlement Work? A Comparison With Anthropological Modes of Adjudication" (unpublished ms., 1979), 13–15.

7. Danzig and Lowy, "Everyday Disputes," 685; Maurice Rosenberg, "Devising Procedures That Are Civil to Promote Justice That Is Civilized," 69 *Mich. L.R.* (1971), 808–11; John H. Barton, "Behind the Legal Explosion," 27 *Stanford L.R.* (1975), 567–84; Thomas Ehrlich, "Legal Pollution," *New York Times Magazine* (February 8, 1976), 17–18; Simon H. Rifkind, "Are We Asking Too Much of our Courts," in National Conference on the Causes of Popular Dissatisfaction with the Administration of Justice, *The Pound Conference: Perspectives on Justice in the Future* (St. Paul, 1979), 52–53; Bayliss Manning, "Hyperlexis: Our National

Disease," 71 *Northwestern L.R.* (1977), 767–82; Ford Foundation, *New Approaches to Conflict Resolution* (New York, 1978), 1–2; Laurence H. Tribe, "Too Much Law, Too Little Justice," *Atlantic Monthly* (July 1979), 25.

8. Austin Sarat and Ralph Cavanagh, "Thinking About Courts: Traditional Expectations and Contemporary Challenges," Working Paper 1979–5, Disputes Processing Research Program (Madison, 1979), 1–9, 81–85.

9. See Isaac Balbus, *The Dialectics of Legal Repression* (New Brunswick, 1976), 17–24; Leonard S. Rubenstein, "Procedural Due Process and the Limits of the Adversary System," 11 *Harvard Civil Rights–Civil Liberties L.R.* (1978), 66–70; Earl Johnson, Jr., *A Preliminary Analysis of Alternative Strategies for Processing Civil Disputes* (Washington, D.C.: Department of Justice, 1978), 2–4, 26–27; Michael L. Rubenstein *et al.*, *The Anchorage Citizen Dispute Center: A Needs Assessment and Feasibility Report* (Anchorage, 1977), 4, 53.

10. ABA, *Perspectives on Justice in the Future*, Report of Pound Conference Follow-Up Task Force (St. Paul, 1979), 296–99; *Pound Conference*, 11; Warren E. Burger, "Agenda for 2000 A.D.—Need for Systematic Anticipation," 70 *F.R.D.* (1976), 92–94; Robert H. Bork, "Dealing with the Overload in Article III Courts," *ibid.*, 232. See also ABA, *Report of the National Conference on Minor Disputes Resolution* (Chicago, 1977), v. Chief Justice Burger has remained an outspoken proponent of arbitration as an alternative to the "avalanche" of litigation; see *New York Times* (January 25, 1982) and, in response, Jerold S. Auerbach, "Burger's Golden Calf," *New Republic* (March 3, 1982), 9–10.

11. Frank E. A. Sander, "Varieties of Dispute Processing," 70 *F.R.D.*, 111–34. For other proposals that tied community courts to the legal system, see Eric Fisher, "Community Courts: An Alternative to Conventional Criminal Adjudication," 24 *American U. L.R.* (1975), 1253–91; John C. Cratsley, "Community Courts: Offering Alternative Dispute Resolution within the Judicial System," 3 *Vt. L.R.* (1978), 1–69.

12. D. I. Sheppard *et al.*, *National Evaluation of the Neighborhood Justice Centers Field Test—Interim Report* (Washington, D.C., 1979), 56; Warren E. Burger, "Our Vicious Legal Spiral," 16 *Judges' J.* (1977), 23.

13. A. Leon Higginbotham, Jr., "The Priority of Human Rights in Court Reform," *Pound Conference*, 91, 107, 110; Laura Nader, Comment, *ibid.*, 114–19; 63 *American Bar Ass'n J.* (September 1977), 1190–91. The following question, posed by Frank Sander, not only demonstrates the creeping legalization of alternatives but their detrimental potential for legal rights. What is the appropriate remedy, he asked, "once there has been informed waiver [of rights] followed by a refusal to go through with the alternative process[?] If that process is arbitration, then, assuming the appropriate state law, presumably an enforceable arbitration award can be

entered." ABA, *Report on the National Conference on Minor Disputes Resolution*, 15. The answer seems likely to require a battery of lawyers.

14. Eric H. Steele, "The Historical Context of Small Claims Courts," *American Bar Foundation Research J.* (Spring 1981), 302ff, 336–43; Barbara Yngvesson and Patricia Hennessey, "Small Claims, Complex Disputes: A Review of the Small Claims Literature," 9 *Law & Society Review* (1974–75), 221–22, 226–28, 256–59; Laura Nader and Christopher Shugart, "Old Solutions for New Problems," in Nader (ed.), *No Access to Law* (New York, 1980), 91–94. (But for a more favorable assessment, see John C. Ruhnka and Steven Weller, *Small Claims Courts* (Williamsburg, Va., 1978), 77–78, 189.) In defense of consumer arbitration, see Mary Gardner Jones, "Wanted: A New System for Solving Consumer Grievances," 25 *Arb. J.* (1970), 234–47; John J. McGonagle, Jr., "Arbitration of Consumer Disputes," 27 *Arb. J.* (1972), 77ff; for a sharp critique, see Aryeh Friedman, "The Effectiveness of Arbitration for the Resolution of Consumer Disputes," 6 *NYU R. of Law and Social Change* (1977), 196–210.

15. Benedict S. Alper and Lawrence T. Nichols, *Beyond the Courtroom* (Lexington, Mass., 1981), 122–23; J. Michael Keating, Jr., "Arbitration of Inmate Grievances," 30 *Arb. J.* (1975), 180; John R. Hepburn and John H. Laue, "The Resolution of Inmate Grievances as an Alternative to the Courts," 35 *Arb. J.* (1980), 12; ABA, *Minor Disputes Resolution*, 20.

16. *New York Times* (July 24, 1981); Alper and Nichols, *Beyond the Courtroom*, 121–22.

17. Paul S. Nathanson and David E. Berman, "Helping the Elderly Cope with Legal Conflict: Alternative Dispute Resolution," Program in the Economics and Politics of Aging, Florence Heller Graduate School, Brandeis University (1980), 1–2; Older Americans Act of 1978, 45 *CFR* 1321.151; Marilyn M. Glynn, "Arbitration of Landlord-Tenant Disputes," 27 *American U. L.R.* (1977–78), 417–18. For an excellent case study, see Mark H. Lazerson, "In the Halls of Justice, the Only Justice Is in the Halls," in Abel, *Politics of Informal Justice*, 119–60. In an attempt to stifle malpractice litigation, more than a dozen states now authorize compulsory arbitration for malpractice claims, a distinct boon to doctors, whose insurance premiums and settlement payments had increased substantially. *New York Times* (January 29, 1979).

18. Indian Law Resource Center, "The Use of Out-of-Court Means for Resolving Indian Conflicts," Preliminary Report (Washington, D.C., 1980), 14–16; Stephen Conn and Arthur E. Hippler, "Conciliation and Arbitration in the Native Village and the Urban Ghetto," 58 *Judicature* (1974), 229–32; Monroe E. Price, "Lawyers on the Reservation: Some Implications for the Legal Profession," 1969 *Law and the Social Order*, 163–64.

19. Indian Law Resource Center, "Resolving Indian Conflicts," 2–8, 14–18; Francis Paul Prucha (ed.), *Americanizing the American Indian* (Cam-

bridge, Mass., 1973), 147–90; Samuel J. Brakel, "American Indian Tribal Courts: Separate? 'Yes,' Equal? 'Probably Not,'" 62 *American Bar Ass'n J.* (August 1976), 1002–6; Price, "Lawyers on the Reservation," 171; James R. Kerr, "Constitutional Rights, Tribal Justice, and the American Indian," 18 *J. Public Law* (1969), 311–38. See, generally, Samuel J. Brakel, *American Indian Tribal Courts* (Chicago, 1978), and William T. Hagan, *Indian Police and Judges: Experiments in Acculturation and Control* (New Haven, 1966).

20. For the evidence, but different conclusions, see Arthur Hippler and Stephen Conn, "The Village Council and Its Offspring: A Reform for Bush Justice," 5 *UCLA-Alaska L.R.* (1975), 22–38, 41–43, 45–55; Conn and Hippler, "Conciliation and Arbitration," 230, 235. Hippler, an anthropologist, and Conn, a lawyer, were primarily responsible for designing the new conciliation procedures.

21. ABA, Report of Pound Conference Follow-Up Task Force, 299–300, 306–9; National Institute of Law Enforcement and Criminal Justice, *Citizen Dispute Settlement: The Night Prosecutor Program of Columbus, Ohio* (Washington, D.C., 1974), 3, 6–7, 29, 37–40; Daniel McGillis, *Neighborhood Justice Centers: An Analysis of Potential Models* (Washington, D.C., 1977), 59.

22. Royer F. Cook *et al.*, *Neighborhood Justice Centers Field Test— Final Evaluation Report* (Washington, D.C., 1980), 4–6, 87–89; D. I. Sheppard, J. A. Roehl, and R. F. Cook, *National Evaluation of the Neighborhood Justice Centers Field Test—Interim Report* (Washington, D.C., 1979), 56; McGillis, *Neighborhood Justice Centers*, 10–12, 32–34, 47–53. McGillis noted the correlation between racial conflict (the absence of community) and origins of the Rochester and Boston (Dorchester) projects; he also suggested that the "system needs to divert cases which are inappropriately consuming criminal justice system time, facilities, and personnel"—a clear indication of the thrust of the early projects (11, 27).

23. U.S. Department of Justice, Office for Improvements in the Administration of Justice, "Neighborhood Justice Center Program," mimeographed release, July 11, 1977, 1–2; Cook, *Neighborhood Justice Centers Field Test*, 13–17, 40–42, 103–6; Wahrhaftig, "An Overview of Community-Oriented Citizen Dispute Resolution Programs," 79–89; Roman Tomasic, "Mediation as an Alternative to Adjudication," Working Paper 1980-2, Disputes Processing Research Program (Madison, 1980), 37–39.

24. Ross F. Conner, *The Citizen Dispute Settlement Program: Resolving Disputes Outside the Courts* (Chicago, 1977), ix; Robert Beresford and Felice K. Shea, "Is There a New Role for Lawyers in Nonadversary Proceedings?" 62 *Judicature* (1978), 50. The phrase "trial by lawyers" is taken from Maurice Rosenberg and Myra Schubin, "Trial by Lawyer: Compulsory Arbitration of Small Claims in Pennsylvania," 74 *Harvard L.R.*

(1961), 448–72. The authors were among the few writers who even raised questions about the second-class-justice aspect of arbitration proceedings. See also Robert Beresford and Jill Cooper, "A Neighborhood Court for Neighborhood Suits," 61 *Judicature* (October 1977), 186.

25. Frederick E. Snyder, "Crime and Community Mediation—The Boston Experience: A Preliminary Report on the Dorchester Urban Court Program," 1978 *Wisc. L.R.*, 742–45, 790; William L. F. Felstiner and Lynne A. Williams, *Community Mediation in Dorchester, Massachusetts* (Washington, D.C.: U.S. Department of Justice, 1980), x, 4.

26. Felstiner and Williams, *Community Mediation*, 3–4, 27–29; McGillis, *Neighborhood Justice Centers*, 72–73. For Middle Eastern comparisons, with an unnamed eastern urban neighborhood that closely resembles Dorchester, see Witty, *Mediation and Society*, 109, 112–13, 125–26.

27. Sally Engle Merry, "Going to Court: Strategies of Dispute Management in an American Urban Neighborhood," 13 *Law & Society R.* (1979), 914–22; Samuel J. Brakel and Galen R. South, "Diversion from the Criminal Process in the Rural Community," 7 *American Criminal L.Q.* (1968), 124–25; Felstiner and Williams, *Community Mediation*, xi, 47–48.

28. For a demonstration of uncertainty about the meaning of "community," and evidence of social control objectives, see McGillis, *Neighborhood Justice Centers*, 44–46, 52–53, 72–73, 121, 128, 136, 148, 155. Among five projects studied, walk-ins constituted 7–20 percent of the disputes; in each project 80–90 percent of the referrals came from criminal justice personnel (p. 39). For a sharp critique, see Richard Hofrichter, "Neighborhood Justice and the Social Control Problems of American Capitalism: A Perspective," in Abel, *Politics of Informal Justice*, 207–43; Roman Tomasic, "Mediation as an Alternative to Adjudication: Rhetoric and Reality in the Neighborhood Justice Movement," Disputes Processing Research Program, Working Paper 1980-2 (Madison, 1980), 51–52, 58.

29. Mauro Cappelletti and Bryant Garth, "Access to Justice: The Newest Wave in the Worldwide Movement to Make Rights Effective," 27 *Buffalo L.R.* (1978), 185–95; Klaus-Friedrich Koch, "Access to Justice: An Anthropological Perspective," in Mauro Cappelletti (ed.), *Access to Justice*, 4 vols. (Aalphen aan den Rijn and Milan, 1979), IV:2–14; Laura Nader and Linda R. Singer, "Dispute Resolution in the Future: What Are the Choices," (unpublished ms., 1975), 2; Tomasic, "Mediation as an Alternative," 8, 19, 26, 27–30.

30. Bryant Garth, "The Movement Toward Procedural Informalism: Politics, Law, and Social Change in the Welfare State," Conference on Critical Legal Studies (1978), 7–19; Richard Hofrichter, "Justice Centers Raise Basic Questions," 2 *New Directions in Legal Services* (1977), 169–72; Tomasic, "Mediation as an Alternative," 52–54, 57–58; Richard L. Abel, "Conservative Conflict and the Reproduction of Capitalism: The Role of

Informal Justice," 9 *International J. of the Sociology of Law* (1981), 249–50, 257–58, 260–63; Abel, "Delegalization," in E. Blankenburg *et al.* (eds.), *Alternative Rechs Former und Alternaven zum Recht* (Opladen: Westdeutscher Verlag, 1980), 27–39, 41–42; Abel, Introduction to Abel, *Politics of Informal Justice*, 6–8.

31. Public Law 96–190, 96th Congress (February 12, 1980); see Paul Nejelski, "The 1980 Dispute Resolution Act," 19 *Judges' Journal* (1980), 290–94; Jerold S. Auerbach, "The Two-Track Justice System," *Nation* (April 5, 1980), 399–400. For the most recent development, a profitable private dispute-settlement service to corporations, see *New York Times* (November 1, 1982).

CONCLUSION

1. *New York Times* (November 23, 1981).

2. Anthony F. C. Wallace, *Rockdale* (New York, 1978), 21. Utopian contractualism is neither logical nor inevitable. The counter-example of Israeli *kibbutzim* (only one among many) is instructive. They offer a fascinating comparative model of non-legal dispute settlement, incorporating many structural similarities with American utopian communities but without any comparable contractual framework. As one veteran *kibbutznik* explained: "the disciplinary tool is the atmosphere which is created by the total community. . . . The individual will either have to change his behavior or leave." Amia Lieblich, *Kibbutz Makom* (New York, 1981), 190. Examples drawn from other cultures reinforce the conclusion that non-legal dispute settlement in the United States has been atypically legalistic, doubtless because American society (which, after all, molded the utopian rebels) is atypically individualistic, materialistic, and competitive.

3. Douglas Hay, "Property, Authority and the Criminal Law," in Hay *et al.*, *Albion's Fatal Tree: Crime and Society in Eighteenth-Century England* (New York, 1975), 13, 27, 33–35, 48.

4. The phrase is borrowed from Robert H. Mnookin and Lewis Kornhauser, "Bargaining in the Shadow of the Law: The Case of Divorce," 88 *Yale L.J.* (1979), 950.

5. Herbert Croly, *The Promise of American Life* (New York, 1909), 136; Marc Galanter, "Why the 'Haves' Come Out Ahead: Speculations on the Limits of Legal Change," 9 *Law & Society R.* (1974), 95–151.

6. Abel, "Delegalization," 34; Abel, "The Contradictions of Informal Justice," 304–6.

7. Laura Nader, "Alternatives to the American Judicial System," in Nader (ed.), *No Access to Law* (New York, 1980), 44, 46, 48–9. "Part of the control inherent in liberal ideology," Professor Nader continues, "is

solving cases one by one rather than making structural changes." Nader and Christopher Shugart, "Old Solutions For Old Problems," in *ibid.*, 64.

8. Robert A. Nisbet, *The Quest for Community* (New York, 1953), 47.

9. Beginnings and endings occasionally converge in curious ways. According to my inscription date (June 1958), I bought and read *The Trial* shortly after I left law school near the end of my first year as a student. I cannot recapture the explicit connection, if any, between my departure and my purchase. Certainly my brief encounter with law had been a form of trial, by ordeal. Perhaps I needed reassurance from Kafka that the legal world I had abandoned was as unsettling—indeed, as Kafkaesque—as my own experience suggested. In a vaguely persistent way that book remained a dim intruder, awaiting an opportune time for rediscovery. The moment came as this book neared completion. For puzzling, but irresistible, reasons I returned to *The Trial*. Once again, it seemed, I needed Kafka's companionship as I made my conclusive break with law. Not until I was midway through my rereading of *The Trial* did I realize the significance of the inscription date: evidently I had to re-enter the bizarre interior world of Joseph K. so that I could finally leave it. I had shared Joseph K.'s anticipation of justice within law. In its absence, however, I no longer wished to share his fate.

Index

Dutch immigrants, in New Amsterdam, 6, 19. *See also* New Netherland

Eastman, Lucius R., 108
Eisenhower, Dwight D., 115
Elderly citizens, alternative dispute settlement for, 127
Enlightenment, 45, 78
Eskimos, alternative dispute settlement for, 128, 129–30

Forward (Yiddish newspaper), 85
Fourier, Charles, 49
Fox, George, 28
Frankfurter, Felix, 89–90, 92
Franklin, Benjamin, 8
Freedmen's Bureau, arbitration tribunals of, 58–60, 66

Gault decision, 126, 127
German separatists, 49
Gideon decision, 126
Goldstein, Israel, and Jewish Conciliation Court (later Board) of America, 82–88 *passim*
Gompers, Samuel, 65
Great Awakening, 41
Greek immigrants, 71
Grossman, Moses H., 106–7

Harley, Herbert, 99
Harmony: balance between conflict and, 37; group, in colonial America, 20, 22, 26–27, 29, 45; industrial, 64; in utopian communities, 25, 52, 53–54, 56; valued by Chinese immigrants, 73, 74; weakening of communal, 40–41

Harmony Society, 51
Harvard Business School, 111
Harvard Law School, 90
Hawley, Joseph, 42
Hay, Douglas, 142–43
Haymarket strike, 62
Higginbotham, A. Leon, Jr., 125
Hoffman, Abbie, 91, 92
Hoffman, Julius, 91–92
Holmes, Oliver Wendell, Jr., 90, 143
Homestead strike, 62
Hoover, Herbert, 109
Howard, O. O., 58–59, 66
Hughes, Charles Evans, 106
Hutchinson, Anne, 22

Immigrant ethnic groups, dispute-settlement patterns of, 6, 69–72; Chinese mediation, 73–76; Jewish arbitration, 73, 76–89 *passim*, 92–93; Scandinavian conciliation, 72–73, 100
Indians, alternative dispute settlement for, 128–29
Individualism, 10, 38, 67, 146; values associated with, 34, 138
Isaacs, Nathan, 111, 112
I.W.W., 98

Jewish Arbitration Court, 81–83, 85, 88
Jewish Board for Justice and Peace, 86
Jewish Conciliation Court (later Board) of America, 82, 84, 85–88
Jewish immigrants, 6, 94; arbitration by, 73, 76–89 *passim*, 92–93
Jewish Ministers' Association of America, 81–82
Judicial activism, 121–22